BIG VOICES

*An Invitation to Women to
Awaken, Increase Joy,
Reduce Suffering, and
Think Differently*

KELLY RESENDEZ

Library of Congress Control Number: 2018930950

ISBN: 978-0-9990461-1-1

First Printing: February, 2018

Published by: 102nd Place, LLC
Scottsdale, AZ

Printed in the United States of America

Dedication

To my amazing children, Paige and Cole;
You have been the best teachers anyone could ever
ask for. I love being your Mom!

TABLE OF CONTENTS

INTRODUCTION

"What we are is God's gift to us. What we become is our gift to God." Eleanor Powell

The moment I realized what God's purpose was for my life I finally knew why I was here. Before that I had achieved what most people would have considered worldly success. I had a wonderful family, a great job, a beautiful home and was socially connected. Still the joy, contentment, and love I expected were missing. I could never relax or stop striving to achieve even more success. I had been guided by my Little Voice or Ego most of my life and could never shut my brain off. The voice in my head was running my life and would never take a break. It took a series of traumatic events for me, and it may for you too, to finally wake up and realize there is something more to life than what we are experiencing. I hadn't been living an authentic life but with faith, commitment, and discipline, I became determined to change. I started on a long journey of self-discovery that rocked me to my core. I questioned every decision I had made and became clear on what I, and God, truly wanted for my future. In doing this, I found my Big Voice.

God has given me the guidance, resources, and understanding to share with you the answers that I found that will lead you to a fuller, more meaningful life. I was called to write *Big Voices;* to take everything I had learned and get louder; to share more, not just locally but as far as I could reach. I cannot promise you that by the end of this book you will clearly know your purpose, but I can assure you that you will feel optimistic, present, and have more energy. You will allow your heart to lead you and prioritize love over everything else. In finding our Big Voices, we must create a social movement where women begin to help one another more and finally live the lives we deserve.

This is my second shot at this book. The first version, a year's worth of writing, was not yet complete when the notebooks that contained it went missing from my home. I will never really understand what happened to them but that became part of my journey of letting go even further. I had to use all my wisdom around forgiveness, trust, non-judgment, and detachment to quickly accept what I could not change and move forward. I would not let this incident steal my joy nor stand in the way of serving God and this movement. After realizing they were likely gone forever, I took a deep breath, put my big girl pants on, and went back to work the very next morning.

In hindsight, it was a blessing to have had the original work lost. I was able to delve deeper and uncover more truths and strength that I didn't know I had. As I was recreating the book, I was tested on my own Big Voice strategies. Over the course of that year, I endured suffering at a level I could not have imagined. My sister's mental health escalated to a point where she is accused of attempting to murder her own daughter while likely suffering withdrawals from prescription psychiatric medications. As I write this she is in jail waiting on psychiatric evaluations to hopefully be moved to a mental facility. I also went through a major realignment at work that caused my worth and patience to be tested. I ended a relationship that I learned so much from. All of these events validated my existing knowledge or created new revelations that would be of significant benefit in finishing this book. My ability to maintain joy while suffering has proven that the strategies do work.

In the last 15 years or so, ever since the internet became a mainstream tool for information, there has been a flood of data on becoming successful, healthy, happy, or fulfilled. But that's just it – we've been inundated with information, more than we could possibly ever read or absorb yet very little of it has changed the quality of our lives; we are actually less happy. Maybe knowing more about what we should be doing to be happier and healthier but then not doing anything has made the problem for us worse. According to Market Data Enterprises the Self-Improvement market is worth 10.4 billion. There is a lot of money to be made from us when we are seeking to distract ourselves and find quick fixes. In this book, we will look at how big businesses and politicians take advantage of us when we are not at our highest capacity or potential. You will be shocked to discover just how manipulative marketing has become and how it supports many of our self-sabotaging habits. Trust me the world doesn't want us to find our Big Voices.

If we know information is not the key to unlocking our potential, what will help us become happier and healthier? What will help us find our highest and most authentic self? It will take learning about neuroscience (how our brain works) and seeing how becoming awake and mindful will allow you to be more intentional about your choices and decisions. You probably don't realize how much of your life is guided by habits and your subconscious thoughts. You need strategies that support maintaining sustainable success knowing you will continue to encounter life changes and challenges.

After you understand your brain and mindfulness better, you will learn the difference between your Little Voice and Big Voice. You'll find that your Little Voice is really your ego; the disempowering thoughts created by your own values and perceptions. Ego is more often associated with men but we all have one. For women, our ego is an accumulation of masks and thinking that creates internal suffering and holds us back from our highest potential. Your Big Voice, on the other hand, is the empowering or authentic thoughts from your soul. You'll also understand how to manage the thoughts that are somewhere in between. These are the thoughts you need to get curious about. Later, I'll give you a "Thought Management Strategy" to help you know the difference and balance these voices daily. Since we all have had PMS we all need TMS to get through our overthinking and hormonal roller coasters.

In the next section, we'll take a deep look at joy and suffering. There is so much in the world that causes suffering but ironically, most of it we bring on ourselves. We will refer to this as self-suffering. As women, we often conspire with one another to make it acceptable to suffer. If you don't have first world complaints about your job, kids, significant other, money, your body, etc., you don't "fit" in most social circles. The reality is these women may feel empty, overwhelmed, or live in fear that they aren't enough, yet they do a phenomenal job of acting happy. Just look at your social media feed and you see it every day. I know this woman very well, because I used to be her. I lived that way until the pain got so great that I had to change. Once I made that decision, God and the universe truly started guiding me where I needed to go.

We are all unique and have been given different talents, emotions, skills, creativity, and passions. Instead of honoring one another we have become divided. We beat one another down, sleep with each other's husbands, and are triggered when other women succeed. We need to wake up and take a stand. We need to experience joy on a deeper level and have clarity while we are here. We need to become pillars of support for each other even if we don't share the same opinions.

In order to do this, you'll need to understand where suffering comes from, the different kinds of suffering, and how our Little Voice plays a role in keeping us there. I'll talk about fear in all its different forms. We'll look at depression and anxiety and how they affect not just our mental state but our physical and spiritual states as well.

A big topic when discussing women's issues is how we "overthink." Literally most of our brains are on fire morning and night. Many of us have allowed our minds to take control and our "overthinking" has stolen our energy and joy. We have gone against our own instincts when we've let our thinking take over causing internal conflict on a major scale. Not only are we not living our best life, but we know it and beat ourselves up daily. We inflict so much of our own suffering just from living in our minds. There are millions of women out there truly suffering at the hand of old beliefs, evil men, physical or mental illnesses, or because they live in poverty. They may have been born in a country or family that believe women lack the same value as men or they were victimized by someone who has made them think they are worthless. These women (and children) need our Big Voices to take a stand and help them.

Once we understand suffering and have made a commitment to live a more authentic and joyful life we'll look at exactly how you start to write a new story. Writing a new story and making the changes you desire takes discipline. It is much easier to be unhappy than joyful. It is easier to hold grudges than forgive others. It is easier to be a victim than a spiritual warrior. It is easier to be passive than passionate. You will be entering a battle between your Little Voice and Big Voice. You will need to be committed to change but not expect your old programming or thoughts to ever go away. You will learn instead how to overcome them and take away their power. Over time, you will step into your true self that is everything God intended you to be. You will also learn how to laugh more and live with less stress.

I'll give you strategies that you can put into place right now – strategies and tools that will make a difference in your quality of life. We will clarify your priorities, create your vision, and determine your goals. We'll also discover things like triggers and how to manage them, why you distract and self-sabotage yourself, and how to overcome it.

Not one of us on earth is perfect. We have all made mistakes and bad decisions. This restorative journey will teach you how to love and forgive yourself for the last time. The world presents enough challenges without you feeling like you are not enough. Get ready to start building that Big Voice and unleash the emotionally successful woman who is going to help change the world one person at a time.

As I said, it is a journey but together we can get there. I've devoted the rest of the book to the tools, techniques, and most importantly, the mindsets that you will need on your journey. You will build a new identity for yourself that allows your Big Voice to guide you. You will learn how to manage overthinking and find peace. You will walk through your pain so that it no longer paralyzes your ability to be present or hopeful about your future. You will step into your purpose of giving and serving God and others at the same time you minimize distractions and self-sabotage. You will learn how to forgive God, others, and yourself. You will wake up, be present, and accept all the beautiful gifts you possess.

I am eternally grateful that I have been blessed with a divine calling to share my knowledge to allow all of us, as women, to live an amazing life. Although this book will not allow my sister to go back in time and avoid all her pain, I hope that anyone else suffering will find these tools and strategies helpful in writing a new story. I know you can become the masterpiece you are destined to be. When you open your heart to God, Spirit, Universe, you can truly heal from your past and face joy despite any uncertainty you have about your future. *Big Voices* will unleash your God-given power and purpose. *Big Voices* will lead you on an incredible journey to become mindful, create a new identity, think differently, and to use your Big Voice to help create more peace and harmony in the world.

Kelly Resendez

MY STORY

"Love is a great miracle cure. Loving ourselves works miracles in our lives." Louise Hay

I am absolutely certain that God never stopped fighting for me. You may call him Spirit, Universe, or God. It doesn't matter. I don't know the actual day it happened but I do know when I finally fell to my knees and surrendered to Him that my life started over. It was as if the mistakes I had made were completely wiped clean and I stopped trying to control everything and everyone.

Looking in from the outside, no one would have guessed that I was suffering. I wasn't being physically or mentally abused. I had a successful career, knew all the right people, and was well liked. I gave speeches and went to parties. I was a workaholic who was fiercely competitive and ultra-materialistic. People thought I had it all. I was obsessed with being relevant. Significance was my idol and I did everything I could to feel important.

I grew up in a small town in Northern California, the child of simple and successful parents determined to make their mark. Although they were in my life, they weren't "present" or intentional about how they were raising me. My mother was especially driven. Looking back, I wish my parents had given me stronger values, had understood that loving me meant they sometimes needed to put me in my place and teach me life's tough lessons. But ours was not a family to have those kinds of conversations and I truly believe they were doing the best they could.

I was born smart, confident, and resilient. I literally thought the world revolved around me. I pushed to be the best at everything. I drove to achieve and relished the attention it brought – the attention I got for an instant as my parents shared my achievements with others. I quickly learned to avoid anything I wasn't good at because my ego was too fragile to take it. I lived to impress. Fortunately, I had a loving, selfless Grandmother who cultivated a sense of compassion in me while I was striving to achieve. Her example saved me from deliberately hurting anyone in my quest to get ahead.

As I shared earlier I have an older sister who

has struggled with her mental health and happiness since I was young. Becoming her savior whenever she was struggling became a huge part of my identity and caused me a lot of suffering and pain. Although I don't blame her for some of my challenges, I have learned how trying to save her, distracted me from my purpose and my own life.

Everything I did was about seeking power and status until one day my life shattered and I realized I was miserable. By the summer of 2002, I was suffering; suffering from a condition of my own creation. I was full of discontent, anxiety, fear, worry, and shame. A trio of rapid events during that time forced me to stop and take a real look at my life. First my 57-year-old mother was diagnosed with dementia. Then I had to sever ties with my sister who was in a volatile relationship and going through a lot at the time. The final straw was my beloved grandmother being diagnosed, and then dying, from cancer within a few short months. The stress was incredible. I couldn't sleep. I was overweight. There was no peace. I could only quiet my brain after drinking several drinks a night. These events became the catalyst for my awakening.

After my daughter was born in 2003, I knew something had to change. I threw myself into searching for answers, the same way I had thrown myself into my work. I started with my physical body, getting my weight and body image under control. Once my body was healthy I had the energy to do the more demanding work of becoming my authentic self. I spent the next fifteen years doing psychology research, attending spiritual and personal growth conferences, and reading self-help books. I became full of wisdom and had all the tools, but it wasn't until 2014 when I turned 40 and I let my walls down and let God in that I truly started to find true peace and joy. This was after my marriage ended and my sister had her first major psychotic break.

My journey before that included the birth of my son, the mortgage industry imploding, my home burning down, a major career change, my mother dying, and my dad having a major stroke. I have had my fair share of life's problems that led me to surrender.

I am a mother, a mortgage industry executive, the author of *Foundation to Sustainable Success*, and speaker. Over the last 15 years I have tried everything and failed many times but I don't regret a minute of any of it. I am so grateful that this journey has led me to my current life.

Throughout this book, you'll read about my internal thought patterns, triggers, and behaviors that have caused me self-suffering. I have since found that these are common amongst many achievers and women in general. I'll reveal over and over how needing to be liked by everyone has often been my downfall and how I was able to push past it.

My life now is filled with love, faith, forgiveness, acceptance, patience, and discipline. It is also filled with lots of laughter. My old patterns and programming still show up trying to push me to revert to past preferences and habits that only created conflict and negativity but my Big Voice overpowers them. I share my story to give you the hope that you can also cultivate a new identity and write a new or modified story for yourself. I know it may sound scary but you aren't throwing away everything. You can keep the parts that you like. We are just ridding ourselves of self-doubt, criticism, worry, shame, pain, anxiety, and fear. Your Little Voice or ego will no longer dominate your thinking or decisions, nor steal your joy.

Now I have purpose and meaning. I live each day with gratitude. The feeling I had years ago of having a calling has been revealed. God has asked me to help other women who might be on the same journey: women who have created their own silent self-suffering. He has helped me find my Big Voice. Through His guidance, I have translated lessons, wisdom and tools from other amazing writers, speakers, and pastors for you to use in your own awakening. He has shown me a path that will bring you joy, excitement, and the certainty that your life is truly guided and divine. Although I am a Christian, this book will help any woman that believes in a higher power. I invite you to come walk this path with me.

"Becoming ourselves means we are actively cooperating with God's intention for our lives. Not fighting Him or ourselves." Stasi Eldredge

WAKING UP

"The biggest adventure you can ever take is living the life of your dreams." Oprah Winfrey

The Big Voices movement is about waking women up and making mindfulness more mainstream. We have to see that most of our life has been guided by our sub-conscious mind and we have not been making the best decisions for ourselves. We have minimized our potential and barely scratched the surface on what we deserve.

We all see hippies and free spirited women living in the moment, but those of us that fall into the over-achiever or productive category cannot imagine living like that. You must admit when you see someone who is so happy and free from stress you want to harm them in some discreet way. We often see being this well-rested and free as impossible. We believe our worth is wrapped up in getting shit done and being busy or productive. This is the largest limiting belief that I see women, who are more driven or more organized, embrace.

We can have it all and achieve balance if we become more mindful and present. My greatest teachers of mindfulness have been Eckhart Tolle, Guy Finley, and Deepak Chopra. They each have a different style of unfolding mindfulness but share the same core belief that our ultimate goal is to be more present.

Wikipedia defines mindfulness as: *the psychological process of bringing one's attention to experiences occurring in the present moment, which can be developed through the practice of meditation and other training.* "Mindfulness" is a translation of the Pali term *sati*; a significant element of Buddhist traditions. In Buddhist teachings, mindfulness is utilized to develop self-knowledge and wisdom that gradually lead to what is described as enlightenment or the complete freedom from suffering. We can live this way only if we rise above our thinking which requires training and dedication.

Through her research, Dr. Shauna Shapiro, a professor at Santa Clara University, found that our minds wander 47% of the time. It is no wonder we cannot remain focused and present, knowing our minds are drifting close to 50% of the time. We can master this drifting by learning mindfulness techniques some of which may be more mainstream than meditation. Trust that you can still become successful, have it all, AND learn how to be more present.

In the next chapter I will introduce a way to do this by describing your highest or present self as your Big Voice and your lowest or unconscious self as your Little Voice. I became more mindful and awake after I accepted there were voices in my head that were imposters. Labeling the thoughts and emotions, these imposters, as my Little Voice made it easier for me to become more selective about what I did with those thoughts and emotions. My Little Voice had been guiding me for far too long when I woke up and realized that it was not serving me. I'll share with you how to listen to your Big Voice and truly create the life you are intended to be living.

The Ugly Truth

Although the women's movement helped us advance our careers, we really haven't come that far. We have not shattered the glass ceiling and there have been significant costs to our emotional and physical well-being. Many women have not found the balance needed to work and raise children. It is rare that you see a woman that has it all and feels great. I am grateful for the movement and have benefited tremendously but we have to be real about how much more there is to do.

We are still the ones that bear the majority of parenting responsibilities and feel like we have to do it all. On top of that, we're made to feel we have to look happy on social media and have children who are perfect. Our fatigue is being taken advantage of by every industry. Politicians and big businesses know how our brains work or don't work when we are overwhelmed. They understand we will spend more, we will eat more, we will complain more, and we will become more controlling. The list goes on and on but the truth is we are suffering.

One reason the women's movement advanced as far as it did was that birth control became legal in 1965 for married couples. Before this legalization it was difficult for women with children to work. It wasn't acceptable to have your children in daycare, and quite frankly there weren't a lot of daycare options around. So women stayed home. Their role was to be in charge of the house while their husbands were the providers. Birth control gave us a choice.

Even today, over fifty years later, controversy continues around birth control. Should employers be made to cover it under their insurance plans?

When can a company object because of its beliefs? In tandem with birth control, and another area of choice, is the abortion issue. If we become aware, we can begin to understand why these two issues are so important. It continues to be about the size of the work force, although the undercurrent is much more subtle. Research proves when women have babies they are less likely to work or become more educated. Are these issues less about women's rights or what is right or wrong morally, and more about big business and government trying to keep unemployment low? We have to wonder if this is really why it is a political issue.

In order to address this, we need to get to the root of the issue. We need to talk to our daughters more and help them understand why it is so important to wait to have children. We have to educate all young people on the consequences of unprotected sex and unwanted pregnancies. Abortion is a symptom of the underlying problem of lack of education. As proof, Jane Fonda founded the Georgia Campaign for Adolescent Power and Potential to improve health and well-being with an emphasis on reducing teen pregnancy. They have since seen a 60% reduction in teen births from educating girls who are in poverty and giving them hope. We have more power when we engage proactively.

Take for example the issue of too many babies dying because of malnourishment many years ago. Rather than deal with the babies' mothers, some smart women determined we needed to educate young girls in rural communities so they were healthy before they became pregnant. This expanded to requiring teachers to gain a better understanding of health and nutrition so they could teach it. Women took a major issue, got to the real problem, and literally solved it. We can do the same thing with abortion if we start looking at the situation differently.

Other issues that we face today in spite of the women's movement include having a lack of balance, abandoning our femininity to get ahead, stress, and fatigue which means our children getting less of our attention because we are so tired. We also have abandoned many community and political issues because we don't believe we are powerful enough to make a difference or are just too exhausted to try.

Let's take a look at some facts and statistics that show just how dire circumstances are in this country:

- Women have failed to shatter in Hilary Clinton's words, "the highest, hardest glass ceiling" and elect a woman as President.

- Women continue to earn at 75% of men in similar jobs. Only one-tenth of all senior leadership roles are filled by women.
- The sexual harassment campaign "Me Too" went viral. A poll by ABC News and *The Washington Post* found 54% of women have experienced inappropriate sexual advances in their lifetime and 30% of women endured it from male colleagues.
- The National Human Trafficking Hotline reports 83% of sex trafficking victims are women.
- According to various reports, currently, the porn industry's net worth is about $97 billion, earned mainly by objectifying women. We could feed at least 4.8 billion people a day with this money. (https://medium.com/@Strange_bt_True/how-big-is-the-porn-industry-fbc1ac78091b)
- Women suffer from depression and anxiety at the highest rate ever. Medco Health Solutions reports that one in four women is given a mental health prescription vs just 15% of men. The National Institute of Mental Health says 21.2% of all women are suffering some form of mental illness. Antidepressant use is up 29% since 2001. Anxiety disorders are the most common

mental illnesses in the US with 18% or 40 million adults suffering from this. (ADAA).

- Market Data Enterprises reports that the drug, alcohol and addictions treatment industry is worth 35 billion. NYT estimated 59,000 Americans died of drug overdoses in 2016, the largest year over year increase we have seen.
- CDC reports that more than one-third of U.S. adults have obesity. Related conditions include heart disease which is also the number one reason women die. Childhood obesity has tripled since the 1970's. Now one in five children between the ages of 6 and 19 are considered obese.
- According to Market Data Enterprises, $60 billion a year is spent on weight loss or gym memberships.
- 12% of kids have ADHD and that number has shot up 43% since 2003 (Journal of Clinical Psychology)
- U.S. Census Bureau shows that 26% of kids under 21 are raised by a single parent of which 82.2% are single moms. Of these single moms, 76% are employed and 30% live below the poverty level.
- According to a joint study Women's Health did with Thrive Global and the American

Sleep Association, 90% of women regularly deal without getting enough sleep. 57% of women lose sleep because of their partners snoring, kids waking them up or animals being hungry. 33% of all women say they never get a good night's sleep. Sleep deprivation is linked to multiple health issues that include Alzheimer's, overall brain health and a lower metabolism. There is no way to know why my mom was diagnosed with dementia in her early 50's, but I can tell you she fell into the category of never getting a good night's sleep.

Although these are just some of the issues we face it is important to note that as women we have so much power to influence them. With our new found mindfulness and some effort, we can change the world. In order to do this, it is helpful to understand why our brains have taken over and caused much of our suffering.

Understanding Your Brain

I am not going to go into a major lesson on neuroscience and how your brain works but I am going to introduce some simple things about your brain that will help you understand why you do what you do OR why you don't do what you should be doing. You need just enough to be dangerous so you have the ability to rise above your own thinking. This will also help you understand why you feel the way you do.

Your brain's main purpose is in keeping you alive and breathing. It is not wired to care about success and happiness and can lead you to make some bad decisions if you don't take your power back. In essence, if you aren't feeling the way you want to be, you can re-program your brain by making some adjustments. When you have a basic understanding of how it works, you will become more aware of how your brain guides your life experiences and decisions without you even knowing it. Becoming awake and mindful will give you more space to see this and potentially change the direction of your life.

Learning more about my brain has helped me make changes that I would not have made other-wise. In addition to taking psychology classes and doing research, the most impactful books that have helped me are *The Female Brain* by Dr. Brizendine, *Upward Spiral* by Alex Korb, and The Power of Habit by Charles Duhigg. Here are some basics that will help you.

We need sleep and lots of it. While we sleep our brain processes information and prepares us to make decisions for the next day; it creates and files memories, boosts our creativity, clears out toxins, and regulates our hormones. According to Dr. Matthew Walker, a University of California, Berkeley sleep researcher, "If you don't sleep, your ability to learn new information could drop by up to 40 percent" Your brain is wired to think repetitively. This is called rumination. Rumination refers to the tendency to repetitively think about the causes, situational factors, and consequences of one's negative emotional experience (Nolen-Hoeksema, 1991). In essence rumination means that it is difficult for your brain to move past something that causes anxiety or concern. Unless you are mindful of this, it may take over. Some people are more prone to rumination than others which can explain some of the reasons for depression and anxiety disorders.

Your brain produces hundreds of neurochemicals and has areas that fire at different times. It performs a variety of tasks that include regulating your body temperature, controlling your motor functioning, and delivering instructions to the rest of your body about what it needs to be doing. Although every part of your brain is important, there are some areas that drastically affect your mental well-being. Your hypothalamus which is part of your limbic system helps you process emotions and is responsible for everything from hunger to how you feel love. It is what releases hormones that are critical to how you feel.

Some of the most beneficial hormones are endorphins, dopamine, serotonin, and oxytocin. There are multiple ways we can increase these: exercise, personal touch, creating goals and taking steps to achieve them, and gratitude. Your gut produces up to 90% of the serotonin in your body which is another reason to keep your physical health in check. Most people aren't intentional about increasing these hormones so they are left searching for happiness in all the wrong places. We will explore this in more detail when we look at suffering.

Your brain is not as complex as it seems but you have to put effort into making it work for you and not against you. The hormone you want to avoid is cortisol which is released when you are stressed. Scientists have found that it can reduce your immune system, increase weight gain, and affect your memory. Cortisol has many other negative physical health implications as well.

Researchers are seeing signs of Neurogenesis, which is our brain's ability to grow new nerve cells when we exercise. Scott Small, a Neurologist and author of *Spark: The Evolutionary New Science of Exercise and the Brain,* shows that just three months of exercise increased blood flow and capillary volume in the hippocampus by 30%. Although complicated, we can see that we have the power to potentially overcome many mainstream diseases just by exercising.

We are different than men and there's no getting around it. In *The Female Brain*, Louann Brizendine shares that the biggest difference between men and women is our hormones. Our delicate balance of estrogen, progesterone, and testosterone isn't anything like our male counterparts and is the reason we shouldn't try and be like men. She shows how the differences can explain questions like: Why are women more verbal than men? Why do women remember details of fights that men can't remember at all? Why do women tend to form deeper bonds with their female friends than men do with their male counterparts? It makes for interesting reading.

Alex Korb, a UCLA Neuroscience researcher, in his book *Upward Spiral* gives us some insight into how our brain affects our emotional state and some tips on making it make us feel better:

Guilt and Shame activate our brain's reward center. Worrying makes us feel better because our brain thinks we are doing something about our problems and can alleviate our anxiety. The reason we feel guilt and shame is because our brain thinks they are good which of course we know is not true.

Gratitude boosts dopamine and serotonin; just trying to find things to be grateful for helps. If you spend more time focused on what you are grateful for you will have more joy. This is such a simple way to feel better and is easy to prioritize.

If you name your negative emotions, it will reduce the impact they have on your overall state. Being conscious of them and labeling them will help so if you are sad say you are sad instead of trying to avoid it.

Start doing goal planning and be more decisive. You will reduce worry and anxiety within your brain if you have a plan. This calms your limbic system. Every decision doesn't have to be right; you just need to be more decisive. You aren't shooting for the best decision but making one that is good enough. Doing this also increases dopamine because your brain knows you have a plan. Setting goals and reaching them is better for your brain then just experiencing good things happening to you. Your brain wants to know you made a goal and followed through on it so it can reward you.

Touch and connect with people more, both physically and emotionally. Relationships and personal touch increase oxytocin which will make you feel great. Give more hugs and get more massages. Massages can boost your serotonin by 30% and decrease your stress hormones. The other area of our brain that is important is our basal ganglia. It plays a huge role in our habit-making behaviors. It helps us develop emotions and patterns. Charles Duhig in *The Power of Habit* says, "the key to exercising regularly, losing weight, raising exceptional children, becoming more productive, building revolutionary companies and social movements, and achieving success is understanding how habits work." He shares we have habit loops that contain a cue, a routine or behavior, and then a reward.

Stress reduces our willpower to overcome bad habits so it is often impossible to stop a bad habit. Duhrig recommends we find replacements for the behavior or routine. If you struggle with self-sabotage regularly the basal ganglia is the area of your brain you can blame. As you become re-warded for something, your brain releases dopamine so it creates cravings for you to seek even more of it in the future. If you look at the worst habits we have: food, alcohol, smoking, and doing drugs, it is easier to understand why they have so much power over us even if we set intentions to quit. The reward circuit is deeply rooted in our brains.

Realizing that you need to take care of your hormones, habits, and that every choice we make affects our emotional and physical well-being, I hope to convince you that you need to be more intentional about how you are living. When we see that everything is interconnected it gives us power over our lives.

"Our deepest fear is not that we are inadequate. Our deepest fear is that we are powerful beyond measure. It is our Light, not our Darkness, that most frightens us."
Marianne Williamson

BIG AND LITTLE VOICES

"There is a Big Voice within every woman, that once found, will change the world." Kelly Resendez

Many people associate having a Big Voice with being outspoken, opinionated, and loud. Someone with a Little Voice might be viewed as meek, mild-mannered, or perhaps shy; a follower not a leader. While this distinction may work when describing personality types, it has no bearing on the way we use our Big and Little Voices to increase our joy, reduce our suffering, and think differently. I will describe them metaphorically as your highest or most authentic self and lowest self respectively, so that one day you will clearly be able to differentiate the voices that you hear every day in your head. Choosing which voice guides you is the most important decision you will make.

Little Voice

Our Little Voice is synonymous with our ego. It is the voice in our heads we have lived with for all of our lives either consciously or unconsciously. It is the reason we have regret. It is the cause of most of our internal suffering. It is what compares us to others either envying them or judging them. It is what tells us there is a hierarchy of people or that it matters what others think. Our ego is what produces all our human preferences that cause us to feel disappointment regularly.

Our ego speaks to us through our Little Voice. It says hurtful things about us and about others. It says things like: we are fat, stupid, ugly, wrinkled, unsuccessful, or unlovable. Then it does an about face and tries to protect us by saying it really doesn't matter, we could change if we wanted to. It is masterful at deceit. It will break us down but then give us just enough to hang on. It is consumed with the past or future and doesn't want us to be present. There are always excuses for decisions made in the past or for why we shouldn't have goals for our future. It knows if we stay present and aware it will lose its power.

Our ego creates disruptions by shifting our focus to perceptions and not facts. It creates opinions about past events and manufactures stories that may or may not be true. All of the thinking or analyzing we do over past situations is an absolute waste of time and energy. If you look back at all the seasons in your life you did this, did it increase or steal your joy, or simply send you on a wild goose chase?

Our Little Voice also tricks us into thinking it cares about our future. The frontal lobe within our brain is overactive and is constantly trying to make predictions to keep us safe and free from being hurt. It is constantly simulating potential outcomes for decisions or events completely outside of our control. Our ego uses this simulator to assess rejection, failure, and frustration in an effort to protect us from disappointment. It keeps us small by pointing out risks and roadblocks that our Big Voice would just push past effortlessly. It is super lazy and uses similar situations we have encountered in the past to make its assessments.

We are unable to predict the future and anticipate what will happen. Our ego though, because it can overpower our true self, will make us believe we can. It convinces us what will happen and then won't allow us to try new things and get out of our comfort zone. Our ego will produce a list of "I can't" or "I shouldn't" statements so if we fail at the very least it will have been right.

Your ego does not desire happiness, peace, or joy. One would think it would, but the fear of failure is too powerful for it to allow you to take massive action. Its primary role is to protect you from becoming the woman God intended.

My favorite acronym for ego is **E**dging **G**od **O**ut. Ego is the opposite of God or love. Any manufactured negative emotion or perception comes from your ego. Although we often think of it as fragile, it is anything but. It is all powerful and consuming unless you make a decision to find your Big Voice. Your ego is not your true authentic self. All fear that is not related to actual life or death situations such as fear of failure or rejection comes from ego.

So why do we have an ego or Little Voice? Many religious or spiritual leaders believe it is the darkness we are born with and must overcome. Other psychiatrists and psychologists believe it is a part of our brain that our personality creates through life experiences. There is no definitive answer and it will forever remain something we cannot understand.

God made each of us unique and gave us the gift of freewill; the ability to choose how to react and respond. We are all born into different circumstances and given different life lessons and experiences. As children, we are all love. We only want our basics needs met. Picture yourself as a baby. You wanted food, love, and a clean diaper.

You weren't yet thinking there was anything wrong with you. At some point though, your ego is formed and starts talking to you without you realizing it is not your highest self. It goes with you wherever you go assessing how others feel and what you should do next.

Depending on your parents, environment, and upbringing your mind or ego eventually takes over in an effort to defend you from hurt or disappointment. Your mind sees those emotions as bad and will make every effort to stop you from feeling them. Unfortunately, your mind doesn't prioritize love as much as it does survival. It also prioritizes preferences that it has created and is constantly guiding you by producing endless thoughts to make decisions based on those preferences.

There are very few people that don't have a restless mind. Our thoughts consume us. I believe that thinking too much and overanalyzing is one of our greatest addictions causing more suffering than anything else. Why our mind thinks it needs to do this is a mystery. The worst part is most people don't want to overthink but are powerless to stop it. We continue negative thought patterns by trying to think less and then beating ourselves up when we do.

One of the primary preferences that our ego

creates is that of perfectionism. In terms of our Little Voice, perfectionism means caring about other people's perception of us more than our own feelings of self-worth or love. When we look at our lives and see that what people have said or done to us has had a massive effect on our emotional state, then we know our ego has been in control.

This false perception of self will also keep us from forgiving others. It will store the pain and resentment that anyone has caused. It will say things like, we have to be strong and tough. We don't need that parent, person, spouse, child, etc. They don't deserve our forgiveness. What ego doesn't tell us is how it uses that pain to hold us back from joy. It also keeps us from being grateful for how God showed up and helped us through the situation.

To recap, your Little Voice or ego is your own private enemy or imposter. If you desire true joy and a deep connection with your Creator, it will try and keep you from it. It will manufacture thoughts and emotions that won't allow you to reach your goals. It will keep you in constant competition and judgment with others. It will place self-doubt and anxiety within you, making you question that you are a masterpiece and deserve all the blessings you have. It will keep your heart closed and not allow you to forgive others. It will also keep you from taking chances and writing a new story.

Although it seems like your goal would be to kill or fight your ego, this is impossible. Your goal now is to accept it, become aware so you have the power to quiet it, and not allow it to guide you.

Many "Type A" women get frustrated that they cannot control their Little Voice once they are aware of it. Trust me, after spending ten years frustrated over my active and always thinking mind, I finally surrendered that all the wisdom in the world couldn't make it go away. I literally tried everything until one day I came up with the best way for me to handle it, which was saying, "Thank you Little Voice. I see you are trying to protect me, but I've got this. God has me protected and armed." Just overriding the voice with my faithfulness has quieted it down tremendously.

Big Voice

Now that you are familiar with your Little Voice and how to spot thoughts or emotions keeping you from being your highest self, it's time to understand your Big Voice. It is also known as your soul's voice. The voice of God or the universe placed in you; your confident and authentic self, or the spiritual warrior within you. Whatever you call it, it exists!! It is guided by instincts, patience, kindness, and compassion and only sees you as the masterpiece you are.

It seems odd that so many of us are trying to find our Big Voice. I have been on this spiritual path for close to 15 years and still have to look every day. Why, I wonder, didn't God make it easier to find? Shouldn't we have come with an instruction manual? With the advances made in the world, why are people not happier? Also interesting is what brings us to this quest over and over again. It might be pain and suffering or just a subtle nudge coming from God. Deep down most of us know there is more to life and have a longing to experience something different.

Your Big Voice is clear on what is important in life. It wants you filled with faith, purpose, joy, and unconditional love. It loves and forgives you for your imperfect ways and knows you are God's masterpiece. It is free from self-created suffering and only produces a deep dependence on God. It has no attachment in this world. It believes heaven will last an eternity and we will all be together again. It experiences grief and sadness, but turns to God for comfort. It accepts the brokenness in this world and knows problems are unavoidable.

We were born into this world with a Big Voice; a purpose that was placed there by God. He has given us each a different puzzle. Some will take longer to uncover their Big Voice than others. Listening to Oprah Winfrey's story one would think she was a lost cause; born to a single, teenaged mother, sexually abused, living in poverty; she faced the impossible and should not have become a success. Instead she has created unimaginable goodness and love in this world. There are others who were born with all the love and support they needed, who have simply stayed in their own suffering and never made a difference.

When we are children we know our Big Voice and are free from self-suffering but somewhere along the way we begin to lose it. The timing is different for each of us because we are all born into different environments. On this journey, it will be important to find our true self rather than our environmentally created self.

It begins at a young age when people start often unconsciously hurting you by making comparisons or disempowering statements. Over time, these comments lodge into your personality, effectively placing a buffer against your Big Voice. If you divide personality into four basic types, the significance driven or confident kid, the shy or timid kid, the lighthearted or funny kid, and the angry or negative kid, you start to see how these children might stray from their authentic self.

The significance driven or confident kid craves attention and importance. They see a big world out there and truly want to be valued and important. As they begin to attract attention they crave it more. They start to try and get more of it intentionally. They lose their authenticity because they are trying so hard to be noticed.

I was this kid with an ego that craved attention; always going above and beyond. I received accolades from teachers and heard I was smart. Helping my grandma with community service often landed my photo in the newspaper. I stunned my parent's friends by knowing so much about politics or world events. I knew sports facts which got me connected with my dad, and I shared my opinions with friends which got me a following. I wanted to be a leader and my young-self felt I had to become someone I wasn't to get the significance I craved. I had no idea that gaining significance would become a habit for me because I craved the reward of being praised all the time. All this work pushed my Big Voice lower and lower so I really had no idea who I was until I finally woke up decades later.

The shy or timid kid has a much different experience. Shy or passive people don't associate with having big egos, but this is far from the truth. They also create a false self, but for a different reason. They are afraid of people or attention and instead of expressing themselves they go inside. The majority of their thoughts never pass their lips. Pain stores much easier into their pain bodies because that energy is never released. This shy kid may have others that are loud or significance driven around them and they simply don't want to compete for attention. They become super internal and are likely to "kinda show up" until they eventually break, releasing all of their pent up pain.

They are not to be confused with a peaceful and quiet person. If you have ever heard spiritual teacher, Eckhart Tolle speak, you know he comes across as meek. The difference is that he is not in conflict about his demeanor. If he has something to share he speaks it. The shy or timid person I am talking about does not speak out but stores up energy as pain or suffering.

The lighthearted or funny kid is the most grounded of the four. They seem to effortlessly get through childhood by trying to stay neutral. They are praised by parents and teachers for their kindness and start to take on the role of the "perfect" kid. Their significance driven counter-parts steal all the attention because the lighthearted kids don't seek the spotlight. The challenge here is often they become afraid to express themselves, to not be the perfect kid, so they lock parts of themselves away by caring too much about what others think.

The angry kid or troublemaker releases their negative energy and creates drama everywhere they go. They are often behaviorally challenged. They aren't born this way, but are shaped by their environment. These kids get triggered easily and don't manage their emotions well. They often crave control and when external conditions aren't right they lose it. Blaming others and shifting responsibility comes easy. Their ego gets the quick release it wants by exploding. Then it rushes to protect itself by creating a long list of justifications. The angry kid who becomes an angry adult passes that pain from generation to generation.

There are many other personality types but I think you can see the point of how, depending on their environment, a child's personality growing up can shape their ego or Little Voice. It is also easy to see how negative self-talk started since you were trying to fit into social norms.

Identifying with any personality type and saying "that's just how I am" will only delay your awakening. You have to get curious and want to learn about you to recognize you weren't always being yourself. Many therapists will charge you countless dollars to analyze your childhood and identify where pain lies under the surface. The challenge is your ego can outsmart you if you aren't clear on your goals going into therapy. You have to make the decision to disassociate with your Little Voice and approach your past with curiosity instead of excuses or blame. You have to find your Big Voice and truly believe you are worthy of living an extraordinary life. Always remember your Big Voice is in the present where your Little Voice dwells on the past or stresses about the future.

Your Thoughts in Between

As you separate the thoughts and emotions you have and are more selective about which ones guide you, you may find some thoughts are confusing. In between our Little Voice or ego thoughts and our empowering or Big Voice thoughts are what I call the thoughts in between. These are thoughts and emotions that don't seem to fit either category. Their value is that they might leave us clues to what's holding us back or what is causing some of our triggers.

They come out of nowhere and often don't make sense. They can be a reaction to what someone said or did. They trigger an emotional response that may create sadness, frustration, or anger. When you aren't quite sure your thoughts are coming from your Big Voice but are also not entirely sure they are coming from your Little Voice, they are curious thoughts.

I store these up to explore at a later date. Getting to the root of why your mind is producing certain thoughts is important, but not absolutely necessary. For example, my intention, part of my Big Voice, is to remain focused on a particular goal but a thought creeps in that says life is going by too fast maybe I should do XYZ instead. This is a curious thought. I don't have to immediately act on it. I can put it away to examine later. Why is it questioning my Big Voice? Is this thought trying to keep me distracted and wedded to old patterns or is it my truth?

These are thoughts where you simply say, "Hmm . . . it's interesting that I keep feeling this way. Right now I need to stay focused on what I need to do, but I am committed to considering this later." You aren't storing these thoughts as resentment, pain, or avoiding their existence. You simply put them aside to work them out later.

Navigating Your Little and Big Voices

To win the battle between your Little Voice and Big Voice is to realize that you are not your thoughts and you must be more present to rise above your thinking. I'll talk about this more when I dive into thought management. For now, it's important for you to begin to recognize when you are hearing your Little Voice versus when your Big Voice is speaking.

I like to create a list with two columns. I put Little Voice on one side and Big Voice on the other. Then I write down all the words, thoughts, or emotions I feel and based on what I've learned about how they are produced place them in either the Little Voice or Big Voice column. That way, when I do hear the voices, I already know which voice is talking. Some examples might be:

Little Voice: No one does it as well as I do. What is wrong with them?
Big Voice: Everyone is unique and different and I am not better than anyone else.

Little Voice: It is impossible to balance it all.
Big Voice: I am in balance when I am clear about my priorities and present wherever I am.

Little Voice: I am scared and don't want to fail.
Big Voice: Life happens outside my comfort zone. I need to take calculated risks. Failing is not trying.

Little Voice: If they hadn't done that everything would be okay.

Big Voice: I blame no one and take responsibility for my life.

Little Voice: I am never going to get healthy, this is just who I am.

Big Voice: Every day is a new opportunity to make new choices. I can do whatever I set my mind to and get healthy.

Accepting you are not who you thought you were is the scariest and most liberating awakening you will have. The person that hurt others or yourself is just a false self your ego built to protect what it feared or to meet its human preferences. It made really bad decisions and closed off your heart to God to do His work. It was controlling because it thought it had to be. You now know that anything that is not joy, hope, or peace is produced from your Little Voice. Although we will still have triggers and might still suffer, we can see the distinction clearly between God's goodness and our own patterns of thinking. Understanding the formation of your false self and why it was created allows you more power to choose which voice you will listen to.

Consistently choosing the right thoughts, the

thoughts that come to us from our Big Voice, is not as simple as flipping a switch. It takes practice and vigilance. It took me years to get to this place and there are still times where old thoughts and patterns lure me in. Being selective about my thoughts was work until I created a process called the Thought Management Strategy which I'll talk with you about in the next chapter. Part of why you needed to learn about your brain is to understand that you have deep thought pathways you have made into habits in your life. Your brain is rewarding you for continuing to use those habits. When you decide to manage your thoughts, you are not only making a decision to think differently but also overriding deeply engraved habits you have had forever.

Why We Need More Big Voices

As I shared earlier, the world is suffering. We are not living in harmony with one another and things appear to be getting worse with our physical and emotional health. If women come together more and see how we are being taken advantage of when we are not fully awake, we can make a huge difference. It will require the restoration of femininity and a major social movement. Many women have abandoned their femininity without even realizing it. We didn't learn how to be after the last major women's movement. We lost a lot of our authenticity because we became controlling, imbalanced, and lost much of our nurturing nature especially within the work place.

I look at masculinity and femininity as a spectrum. We all have a mixture of both, but one is typically more dominant. Most women are more feminine and most men are more masculine. Identifying where you fall on the spectrum is a process and will take time. You will be peeling back layers of ego to find your truly authentic self. You will need to notice each day what you did and how it made feel, to better understand what brings you joy and meaning. Wikipedia describes femininity as: *gentleness, empathetic, compassionate, sensitive, caring, tolerant, and nurturing* whereas masculinity is: *courage, independence, and assertiveness*. Neither are bad unless you are giving up your true essence to try and be something you are not.

As women have entered the work force in larger numbers it seems more of our masculine sides have emerged. We have left behind much of our nurturing and caring qualities and traded them off for advancement and stature. We have sold our authenticity to achieve our goals.

It doesn't have to be this way. Our natural

tendencies and strengths can create a leadership style that is just as effective. Understanding how others perceive situations can bring about change that can't be achieved by just making your own goals. We need to bring more of our feminine into the workplace because it will change the world. We need more businesses that are consciously trying to make a difference versus just trying to maximize profits. If we are more feminine with a Big Voice, we will speak up and demand more for ourselves. Whether it is the environment you work in, the wages you earn, or the impact you are making, uniting in our Big Voices will move the needle.

Our challenge is in trying to be pleasing rather than acquiring more skills and wisdom and standing on our own efforts. We sit back and wait for someone to validate us instead of having the self-confidence to know we are crushing it. No one else can generate our joy or energy. It must come from within.

I'm not saying that the masculine energy that exists within us should be ignored. Directing it will enable us to take massive action against businesses or industries that are hurting our world. We might feel like companies are leading us in the wrong direction, but then we don't stand up and do anything. Take the food industry, for example.

Women are responsible for buying a majority of the food, yet we continue to allow them to fill it with sugar, pesticides, hormones, dyes, preservatives, or other additives that are not healthy. Out of convenience or laziness, we allow ourselves and our families to consume things that are addictive (sugar/carbs) and provide no nutritional value. Maybe we don't think the big names will listen to us, but they don't need to listen. If women used their Big Voices and quit buying so much processed food filled with crap, the companies would be forced to either change it or stop selling it. Supply and demand rule the business world and we simply need to rise up and demand better health for our families.

Willpower won't work. We know that it is not enough to overcome deeply formed habits most of us have had for years. Obesity rates in adults and children have soared. We can wait until poor health is an epidemic or we can rise up with our Big Voices and demand higher standards. We are the ones with the most power over our choices and our children. We cannot continue to sit back and be self-loathing. Caring about our kids is not letting them do what they want. If it were up to them they would be on social media, watching TV, or playing video games while eating junk food and sugar all day.

As a united force, women are so powerful. We can change an entire nation or world if we have the right vision and don't sell our souls. The whole purpose of *Big Voices* is to encourage you to become strong enough to stand up for what you believe. We need to use both our masculine and feminine energy intentionally. When we get so wrapped up in emotion or feeling, we can become passive or overwhelmed. It is okay to use our masculine energy to push through this and get things done that matter. The reason so many women become more outspoken and generous in their early 50's is because their hormones no longer rule their life. Estrogen goes down and testosterone goes up which naturally allows us to speak the truth more. We need to be more intentional and disciplined in spite of our hormonal fluctuations. We have the power to override our patterned behavior and stick to our mindset.

There are so many beautiful gifts of being feminine that are purposeful. Having the ability to relate to others and be empathetic is a gift. We can often feel other people's pain which allows compassion to flow. This has to be balanced with not trying to fight other people's battles or we can lose ourselves.

I recently attended a close friend's funeral who was taken early from this world. He shared with me years ago after he knew he was terminal that he wanted to leave a legacy here on earth. As people poured out their stories about Jon and his work in the addiction community, it sank deep into my soul that his legacy will live forever. When we think about finding our Big Voice, we not only want to find love and truth, but also our purpose in this world. With our different gifts we each have the ability to impact the world and leave a legacy.

We will not do this if we are focused only on ourselves. We will not do this if our cup is empty and we are worn out. We will not do this if we believe we only have the capacity to focus on work, or our families, and nothing else. We are designed for so much more and we must seek out both our purpose and the energy needed to maintain it.

Jon had been in recovery for over 20 years. He dedicated his life to researching and educating the community on the neuroscience behind addiction. He defined some of our human needs that may not have been met early on and the cravings those needs could produce. Every last drop of wisdom he had was left for the world to retain.

When you look at your own life you have to

ask, "What will my legacy be? What will people say about me? Will I stay in people's hearts forever? Do they know how much I love them?"

You must live this life fully to leave a legacy. You don't have to touch thousands like Jon did to live an extraordinary life, but you must discover what is burning in your heart to share. It might be love and compassion. It might be to stand up against poverty or abuse. It might be to overcome your own shame so your story gives others hope.

Finding your Big Voice isn't just about self-improvement and reducing your own suffering. It is about taking what you've learned and increasing joy within you and around you. Just becoming your authentic, truth-speaking self will help other women do the same. We have all met women we admire that are true role models. We need more of them raising children and standing up for women around the world that don't have a voice. Many of us were born in warm homes with plenty of love, but so many women were not. The poverty and evil that exists in the world is overwhelming. Young children are being born every day into incredible circumstances we can't begin to imagine. If more of us rise up against everything that is in opposition to love we will impact the world. We will harmonize communities and give them hope again.

We can stay safe in the bubbles we have created or make a decision it's time to do something. Many of us have been passive, especially if we are trying to juggle self-care with work, kids, or family. The enemy of leaving a legacy is that we will seek our purpose tomorrow. Time then flies and not only have we not lived an extraordinary life, but we also have guilt and shame for it. I urge you to start simple. Listen to the needs of your friends or community. Take some time alone to just feel some subtle calling to help others. If nothing comes, simply start donating time or money to different causes. Volunteer at church to serve. Ask your friends if they have anything they need help with.

My impact is wide. I show up to minister whether I am at work, home, or a cocktail party. I believe God leads women to me because they need joy, wisdom, and love. I simply show up every day with the intention of being a servant and let my day take me from there. Trust that if you show up with your Big Voice more, you will be guided to help others.

Your Big Voice may guide you to fight hunger, animal cruelty, social injustice, sex-trafficking, or volunteer at the library. There is no right, wrong, or one size fits all. Each of us has a unique purpose and as long as we leave a legacy of love and meaning we have lived an extraordinary life. I urge you to go deep and realize that without us things will only get worse. We need to be role models for generations to come. I ask you to join me and rise up against the suffering that humans create.

"We realize the importance of our voices only when we are silenced." Malala Yousafzai

THOUGHT MANAGEMENT STRATEGY (TMS)

"A journey of a thousand miles begins with one step."
Lao Tzu

One of the key elements in allowing our Big Voices to be heard above the constant yammering of our Little Voices is to manage our thoughts better so they don't control our action or guide us into inaction. No one ever taught us that our thinking is what guides us to joy or suffering. Mindfulness was not taught in schools so most of assumed all the voices were our own. I was taught it was my "choices" that were important. The struggle is that our repetitive thoughts are what can control our choices and bring us great emotional distress. You learned in the last chapter that your ego is what produces the majority of your thoughts. These thoughts are not a part of your true authentic self but rather are predictable patterns from your past. You are not your thoughts as so many people believe, but as Eckhart Tolle coined it, "You are the watcher of your thoughts" when you are awake.

Though we may not be able to understand why we have so many thoughts or where or why thoughts come, we must learn to accept they are a part of our lives and have the power to cultivate or steal our joy. It is important to have thought mastery if we are to live an extraordinary life.

Gaining control of how your thoughts impact you requires dedication. There are a few things you need to know to before you get started. My first warning about this process is that it initially takes lots of energy. You may grow fatigued as you become more conscious of all the thoughts you are having. Ultimately, the end goal here is to quiet negative thoughts from your Little Voice and raise your Big Voice up so you can create the life you really want. As your brain is re-programmed, the effort you will need to manage your thoughts will decrease.

The first year after starting my mindfulness practice, I was having two thoughts instead of one all day long. For a period, I hated Eckert Toole for waking me up. I had the first thought and then a follow up thought questioning where the first thought came from. It was exhausting asking me all day if I was present but trust me it gets easier when you set the intention to not think so much and be wherever you are.

My second warning is that you must have self-love and compassion. If instead you start feeling regret, fear, or shame for how you lived before, STOP! You need to cultivate more confidence and acceptance that your life has unfolded exactly how it was supposed to. As your ego loses power it will try all its old tricks every step of the way to stop you from changing.

My third warning is to come to this process without expectation. You simply want to make the decision that your thoughts and emotions won't rule your life. The second you expect anything from the process you will become disappointed. Your sole purposes should be to spread love and joy, so just watch for those occurrences when you do and celebrate them daily. Your focus should be gratitude for becoming aware, not on expecting anything in return. You must learn to laugh at yourself or this process will be too heavy for you.

It is important to remember this is not a quick fix. It takes more awareness to be conscious than unconscious. You will have more joy and impact if you live an intentioned life. However, you may be lonelier on this journey for a bit. Others may not be where you are and you need to accept them, imperfections and all. Resist the urge to compare or share the TMS strategy unless they have given you permission.

Let's dive into the Thought Management Strategy (TMS) that will help you. First I want you to just stop and breathe for five minutes. As you breathe in say Big and as you breathe out say Voices. When you focus on your breath and intentionally say these words, you will see that no other thoughts come at the same time. Nothing comes. This illustrates that when your Big Voice is in control your Little Voice ego is quiet and separate from you.

We cannot stay in this meditative state forever, so now sit for five minutes with no focus on your breath or intentions. Just sit. As thoughts start coming at you, try to visualize them metaphorically. You might see ocean waves, floating clouds, assembly lines, or any other constantly moving metaphor. I see my thoughts that come from my Little Voice as circus monkeys that show up in my brain. I visualize them hanging from the ceiling, opening up drawers, throwing stuff, and being naughty. Notice as you sit that you aren't creating the thoughts, you are just watching them. I have found when I think of them as funny it makes the process easier. Some thoughts won't make sense and others will. There is no right or wrong to what you think. Some might be thoughts about what you need to do, who you need to talk to, issues that are going on, or a myriad of other things. Some of them may be negative thoughts and that is okay too. There is no right or wrong. Have compassion for the craziness your thoughts bring you.

While you watch your thoughts, begin to sort them like you are doing laundry. Little Voice or ego ones go to the "don't need you" pile. Choose not to react emotionally or physically to them. If you like, you can thank your ego for manufacturing them. I sometimes will say, "I appreciate what you are trying to do, but today I choose joy and love." Your Big Voices thoughts go into the "take action" pile.

Thoughts in between are acknowledged and can be looked at later. It often helps to write these thoughts down. Maybe metaphorically these are items you will hand wash and do later. An example would be you need to talk to your boss about how he just treated you. You have a thought it is time to find a new job and want to react by quitting. Rather than do that you take the time you need to respond and think about this later. We never want to be passive in life, but it does help to be strategic. Giving the thought space will allow you to devise a solid plan for dealing with your boss. I will actually say to my thought of quitting, "Thank you. That's an interesting one. I will spend some time on that later."

Your Big Voice thoughts are action-oriented and purpose-driven thoughts that bring you closer to God and your goals. They come from deep within you and are aligned with your values and priorities. These thoughts can help build your confidence and enthusiasm about life. They are the ones you do something about. Examples would be new ideas for a project, clarity around decisions regarding your personal life, work, or your family, or intuitive thoughts about your future and what you can do today. These thoughts also accept you might not feel like doing everything you should be. They can override laziness, boredom, or fear, and push you to do things you may not want to but should be doing.

I experienced this recently after a long day. I was lying in bed with my son and a thought popped up that said I should get up for as long as I could and do some exercises. My goals are that I do exercises three to five times a week, but I honestly was beat. Although I felt exhausted, my Big Voice thoughts empowered me to take action. Trust me my Little Voice chimed in and said it was no big deal and I could do more tomorrow but I chose to listen to my Big Voice. I didn't get a full hour of intensity training, but I did get 15 minutes of strength and core training done. You see if I had lain there those 15 minutes I would have received nothing sustainable nor felt good. I would have felt lazy. Instead, I went to bed feeling strong and confident I have the power needed to live an extraordinary life. As I will share later my workouts are anything but traditional and are done at the most random times.

Even when you have mastered TMS, and have a better grasp around choosing the thoughts you allow to influence you, the circus monkeys (Little Voice thoughts) can still attack. When you are tired or worn out, they are more likely to run rampant and create fear, anxiety, regret, or shame.

I have a strong handle on my thoughts, but if I have too much uncertainty in my life I tend to get triggered by other people more easily. I will focus on the faults in others and my thoughts will cause doubts about my life. Am I really in the right relationship? Am I truly capable of managing my purpose and priorities? Should I leave my job? Are my standards for a relationship too high? Should I just order a husband from another country? (Actually I have not had that one but why don't women do that too?) It happens quickly. I can be content and at peace one minute, then something gets said or something happens that triggers me, and my circus monkeys can quickly take over.

I have never been able to kill my monkeys. Trust me I have tried. I have visualized taking a machine gun and lining them up like they do in the movies. I can only sit in awareness and laugh at them. I am always humbled by them and reminded that when I am not adequately caring for myself I start projecting. If I am strong enough to override them quickly, I can make a list of my triggers and be decisive. I decide right then if I can avoid the trigger or grow through it. I also assess my own current needs. Usually, when the monkeys show up in multiple areas of my life at once, it's because I am not balancing my priorities. I have taken on too much and my own needs have been neglected.

When my work life is too full, I neglect my body. I don't have enough energy to go to the gym. I also resent anyone else who is stressed. I think my level of stress is appropriate because I have more on my plate and I tend to look down on others. I also find myself resenting others who do have the energy to go to the gym or workout because they don't understand how much harder my job is than theirs. When someone complains about driving their kids to soccer practice, I want to rip their head off. When I get into this hole I become irritable and distant, but am still able to control my behavior. Obviously all of the thoughts that my life is harder than anyone else's are ridiculous and I realize after I am through feeling sorry for myself that my Little Voice had taken over. Fortunately, because I have been practicing TMS for a long time, I am aware of the devastation it could cause if I transferred my emotions around these thoughts to others. When this happens, I turn to writing in my journal because I take responsibility for my monkeys who want to lash out and push others away. I simply pray for God to come and fight this battle for me.

Having self-compassion is critical when we cannot perfectly manage our thoughts and be mindful. Thinking about the thinking only makes it worse. I believe so much of our stress and anxiety is created this way. Because you now have a strategy that helps with managing your thoughts it doesn't mean we are exempt from overthinking. Some view our overthinking as an attack and believe we should fight it head-on. Because we cannot control our thoughts this would take a lot of energy leaving us even more exhausted and stealing more of our joy. A better answer is to wait for the storm to pass (or for my wild monkey party to end) while you set strong boundaries and stay rooted in your values.

I can become impatient and irritable when I am in this storm. It's almost like the college party where you were the only one not drunk and having fun but you know you need to stay until everyone is safely home. I pray feverishly for God to intervene and for some of the weight to be lifted. I cannot ask myself, "Why me?" or I will drop into self-pity. I simply accept this is a part of the human experience and set my intentions to stay alert so I can manage my thoughts better.

You have decided to do two things when you make a commitment to think differently. One is to feed yourself new things to think about and the other is to manage the thoughts that still come that you have no control over. TMS won't work if you only do one or the other. The pathways formed throughout life are deep and might be feeding needs your ego has created. You must override these thoughts by making other wisdom you have acquired more pronounced. For example, if the thought is, *it won't matter if I eat that because I am fat anyway and will never get healthy,* then leaving yourself a gap between the thought and the action can help you override it with new wisdom that says, *I am amazing and beautiful. I will only feed my body healthy food that helps me achieve my health goals.*

As you practice TMS you will start to see how simplistic and repetitive your ego or Little Voice thoughts really are; telling you the same stories over and over, trying to guide you to make bad decisions. Thoughts are habitual. The key to living an extraordinary life filled with peace, love, and joy lies in managing your thoughts. Being mindful and conscious that your highest and most authentic self is always there within you and you are so powerful you can quiet your Little Voice will give you the confidence you need to start thinking differently.

On my website, www.bigvoicesrise.com, you will find a Thought Management Strategy that will help you create new thought patterns around the challenging areas in your life. You can document thoughts that are reoccurring and develop new thought patterns to override them. It seems too simple that we can change our life by just thinking differently but it is true.

"We don't see things as they are; we see them as we are."
Anaïs Nin

JOY AND SUFFERING

"When the mind is pure, joy follows like a shadow that never leaves." Gautama Buddha

We all want to experience more joy, yet we must recognize it takes time and attention. We know how to have fun or be happy for short periods of time, but not create a sustainable deep feeling of joy. Joy should be a constant state we feel "in spite of" anything that happens in our life. Joy keeps us armed against triggers or situations outside of our control. Unlike energy, joy is not something we need to cultivate, but rather is something that exists in us already that we can tap into with guidance. God has given us this source that we can call upon when we need it. Unfortunately, our Little Voice does not want us to find joy and will try desperately to keep us from it. Our Little Voice wants us focused on ourselves whereas our Big Voice knows our joy comes from focusing on God and love.

Joy lights up a room and speaks the truth. Joy is not delusional about one's circumstances, but has surrendered any outcome to God. Joy is living with hope and faith regardless of our circumstances. It fully believes that everything happens for us and our life is guided. Joy is detached from anything of this earth, has no expectations, and experiences all through love and acceptance.

Joy requires loving and forgiving yourself for past sins or mistakes. It knows if you choose God you are redeemed and can let go of any disempowering emotions such as shame or guilt. Joy knows you are broken and imperfect but has compassion for all, including you, who are suffering. Joy is maintained when you have strong boundaries for the wayward and accept you are not here to save anyone.

Regardless of what you may have thought, joy and suffering are not opposites. You don't get to choose one or the other, but have to learn to live with both simultaneously. Your Little Voice wants you to believe you cannot experience joy while you are suffering. It will guide you to believe that all the "if onlys" are true. If only my husband were more present, then I would be happy. If only my boss saw my potential, then I would earn more and be happy. If only my body looked better, I would be happy. The endless list of "if onlys" in most of your life keep you from seeing your truth is in finding joy in spite of your suffering.

Sure, you have to show up, be disciplined, and stretch yourself to feel successful, but joy comes from a deeper place. It comes from knowing you were created for a purpose and with a purpose. It comes from knowing your Maker knows you inside and out and has been alongside you the whole time. It comes from knowing how loved and chosen you are in spite of anything you have ever done. Joy knows you can be born again and write a new story over and over for as many times as it takes.

I didn't experience true joy until all my walls had come down. It took years on this journey to fully accept my authentic self didn't need to worry about anything. It wanted so badly to cling to old thought patterns that sought perfectionism and significance. It avoided rejection at any cost. I think I held some false belief joy would eliminate negative thoughts or emotions so I had been searching for joy outside of myself. I had days I felt it and days I didn't. Now I have come to accept that joy is messy at times. I wake up filled with it and go to bed with it, but what happens in between can be unpredictable. I have accepted that joy is found within me.

If you accept that today is where you need to focus, you won't weigh yourself down with regret from yesterday, or anxiousness about tomorrow. You can't run and hide from problems or setbacks. They happen no matter how strong or grounded you are. You will experience pain. People get sick, lose jobs, die too soon, lose money on investments, etc. You cannot run from life's turmoil, but you can choose to face it with trust and faith. God doesn't cause abuse or sickness. He doesn't give you what He thinks you can handle or need to grow regardless of what you've heard from others. When you need God, He is always there. He is the constant companion you can call upon when you are in need. That is the truth in how I have experienced it. Many of us need to hit rock bottom before we can rise up and become our biggest and most authentic self. The higher intelligence that has existed in you from the beginning often cannot be tapped until you are in so much pain you have no choice but to find it.

Every day I wake up with the intention of increasing joy, but there are days that get the best of me. I will feel sadness or hurt, but still have a deep knowing that everything will always be okay. It makes it easier that I am a believer and have a strong faith I will spend eternity in heaven. I see suffering here as temporary. This mindset has helped me through this past year as I have navigated the situation with my sister and family. I am so sad that she is suffering and in jail but I can still know that one day our suffering will be gone.

As you set out on this journey to increase joy, realize you may never have tapped into it before. We have all had perfect seasons where everything was just right and we felt so happy. This is not the joy we are trying to increase. It is easy to feel good when life is great. We have to learn how to feel joy in spite of anything. We need to feel it even when none of our human preferences are met and our life is falling apart. We need to feel it when we are lonely and cannot see our future improving. We need to feel it when others disappoint us or abandon us.

It is possible to have the deepest knowing that you are loved completely and are a unique masterpiece in spite of the things happening around you. The world can be falling apart, but you will be able to show up and still be a beacon of love and light. As you start every day, make the intention that no one will steal your joy.

Self-Suffering
Suffering will consume you if you give it a chance.

It's important to explore what it is and how it will steal your joy if you let it. You can never remove bad things happening to you or around you, but you can learn how to experience grief, anger, pain, or sadness and remain filled with joy. When I reference suffering within these pages I am referring to self-suffering and am not talking about the women who have physical or mental illness.

Suffering is the most complicated psychological and spiritual concept to grasp. You can't see it or touch it. Only the person suffering can feel the intensity of its wrath. I used to think only someone with depression, grief, pain, shame, regret, or anxiety was suffering. This was before I became more mindful of how many women struggle with so much more. Making decisions, balancing time and energy, loneliness, self-doubt, and many other situations open the door for suffering. Although it may start as a small wound, it often becomes like flesh-eating bacteria that overtakes you.

We may become powerless to self-suffering if we don't have the tools to counteract it. If we could only stop focusing on it or thinking about it, the suffering would stop. But we are complex, emotional beings so this is not possible.

What can you do to turn suffering into something less negative and gain more power from it? You can get curious about the root causes and evaluate what is triggering you. You can learn from it so you are more prepared for the future. You can address the triggers, something I'll talk much more about in a later chapter, and make decisions to either grow through them or avoid them.

Suffering is a valley of darkness. It can be challenging to see the light or feel optimistic. You can turn your faith to God or the universe to guide you or stay stuck. If you are armed to handle suffering before it happens, you can minimize the intensity and duration of it. What you don't want to do is attack others or make decisions when in this state. Tony Robbins, a noted life and business strategist, describes this state of suffering as a figure eight. Someone can go back and forth from sadness, fear, and hopelessness to anger, blame, and resentment. In essence, you are stuck in an endless loop of negative emotions. Many people disrupt this loop with negative distractions like cheating, drinking, smoking, or gambling. A better choice is to rise above it and create a new way.

I recently got stuck in my own figure eight. Being more mindful and having knowledge doesn't dismiss me from these attacks. I am still very much imperfect. I had a lot on my plate at work and with my kids. There were monster decisions needing to be made and my ego was fighting me. My boss had questioned how I was running things and I didn't feel good about it. Although I was aware of it, I cared way too much about what he thought but knew I was doing the best I could with what the company had given me. I was worn out and beat. Instead of staying on track, I allowed my self-care and compassion to be sacrificed. I suddenly shifted focus to what other people were doing wrong. Small things the people close to me did or didn't do became my focus which in turn made me irritable. I pulled away from those I love. Everything happened quickly. My Little Voice took advantage of my weakness. I felt out of control and anxious. I didn't fall asleep as fast and if I woke up through the night my brain was on fire. Within days, I was ready to run away and buy a tiny house far from civilization.

This episode humbled me yet again. It had been a while since I had suffered that deeply and I had started feeling like I was super-human. I had begun to see my faith as unshakable. Then *BAM!* I was aware I wasn't present and had to force myself to not take my suffering out on others until I got through it. I was triggered more easily and felt lots of "always" and "nevers." Thoughts like *my son never does anything for me* popped up when he threw a fit when I asked him to grab me some dark chocolate after a long day. Granted, he was just as cozy on the couch as I was, but I was so tired. In a split second, I took inventory of everything I had ever done for him and was pissed he wasn't more compassionate and grateful. It was easy to label him as "always" ungrateful. The truth is, I should have expected him to say no and not jump right up. He couldn't feel the fatigue I felt after having to let go of good employees at work because business had slowed down. Subconsciously, I had set myself up. I walked right into a "piling on" situation. It's impossible to avoid suffering because we are human but we can set intentions that we won't allow it to hurt anyone.

When women are stressed, we become more masculine and start suffering even more. We get out of our hearts and jump into our heads. We project easily and focus on other people's flaws with a magnifying glass. We have a tendency to pick and fight more battles. We are not made to be masculine all the time and staying there will steal our joy and energy.

It is so important that we get clear about the difference between standards and preferences. When we decipher the difference we can communicate our needs with clarity and reduce a lot of the suffering we create for ourselves. I relate standards with needs and preferences with wants. Knowing I *need* more certainty in a relationship as my standard is not wrong. *Wanting* my partner to change though is a preference and is wrong. I can grow through preferences, but must set boundaries for standards. Although standards are necessary the goal is not to create long lists of them or we will be constantly disappointed and unhappy.

I have always lived my life with high standards. I love being disciplined and uncomfortable. I love identifying a fear or trigger and finding a way to grow through it. I love helping others do it too. I love having a high bar for myself and being purpose-driven and goal-oriented. My personal self-suffering often comes from my standards being so high that my preferences are impossible to meet. My relationship with my kids, my job, my significant other (when I have one), and my friendships all are negatively affected by this. My work is always to love unconditionally and accept people for who they are. I can become judgmental or hard on those closest to me if the way they show up doesn't meet with my standards or preferences. When I am out of balance and am not meeting my own needs, it is more challenging for me to be accepting of other people's mistakes or imperfections. Once I become judgmental, I then become disappointed with myself and start asking the dreaded "what is wrong with you?" question. It has been a vicious cycle I have lived with for most of my life and something that I strive to overcome daily.

My children are both lucky to be, and burdened with being, my kids. I have given them every opportunity to succeed by providing the best private schools, sports clubs, and support. I have shared wisdom with them about life, the lessons I learned on nutrition, health, and happiness, and the importance of being a believer. I support them with love and encouragement, and yet they still struggle with feeling "not enough" at times. They both feel an unspoken need to be high achievers and take on a lot of pressure.

I recently discovered that because of my success they feel some anxiety already at ages 12 and 14. Some of my intentions to stop them from being like me at their age have backfired. They think I am judging them even when I don't say anything. The affirmations or compliments I have given them created even more desire for them to be what I wanted them to be. I am feeling like a bad mom because of it. You need to accept and understand that external pressure, even if it is unintended, can cause suffering at a young age. Just having them overhear you telling someone else how amazing they are can cause them to believe they need to be amazing all the time which is impossible. By being a more intentional parent you might help keep negative pathways from forming. Instead of wallowing in guilt, I am committed to helping them out of their heads. I think a large part of my challenge is that the self-suffering I experience today started when I was young.

Now my current life experiences fit neatly into these pre-patterned pathways. Knowing my brain is lazy, it will try and generate decisions that are most like I made in the past. I have my perfectionism pathway, my guilt pathway, my health fear pathway, and my relationship uncertainty pathway. I go down these predictable paths as I encounter life until I become awake enough to work through them. Picture yourself driving the same route home every day; you know where to go without thinking about it. This is how it works for us when a situation seems similar to something we have encountered before. Our brain produces similar thoughts and decisions as it did before unless we override it. So if you need to stop at the store you have to leave yourself a note on the dashboard before you end up in your driveway and forget the milk.

I have a very deep pathway regarding relationships with men that has caused me self-suffering. Although I am aware of it, I carry fear and worry about finding the right partner. Either I am disappointed with the men I meet or I am hopeless that I will ever meet anyone that can meet my standards. There are so many emasculated men out there that it is easy to be let down if I focus on it. It causes suffering for me because I want so badly to find peace and contentment within a relationship. With every failed relationship, I have grown personally and become clearer about my needs versus my preferences. I have learned more about myself and healed parts of myself I hadn't known were in pain that may have gotten me into the wrong relationships before. Unfortunately, I have chosen to be with men that don't have the same standards or drive that I do, so I end up creating my own figure eight of emotions. I love so many things about them, but then my deep craving for them to be a provider or more driven kicks in. I go back and forth from loving them to questioning our compatibility. I try my hardest to push through these challenges, but I have accepted some of my needs are just too deep in my heart. I have now accepted I need to be patient and wait for God's divine timing versus trying to settle for a relationship that creates suffering for me.

Accepting that our heart has deep desires can help us suffer less. We have to quit beating ourselves up for longings we may not have any control over. As women, accepting we want to be chosen and fought for is okay. If you have a calling or desire, you owe it to yourself to follow it and not settle in any area of your life.

The Buddha believes no human is free from suffering or unhappiness. He believes the root of all suffering is a desire for material things or to remove things we dislike. His recommendation is that we need to strive for nirvana or inner peace. He believes we will continue to be reincarnated until we find it. As I find myself caught with discontentment, I giggle and say, maybe in my next life.

I have given up my freewill to God and am patiently waiting for his guidance during this season. I know He knows I am struggling with sadness and will reveal His plan for me. I am self-compassionate that no matter how wise I am, I can never avoid suffering. All I can do is wait out the storm and not take it out on the people around me.

The truth about suffering is simple. The more you focus on it the deeper the pathway gets. The longer you focus on it the deeper it gets. As we learned earlier, what you think your brain drives deeper into you as you sleep. And even after the root of the suffering is gone, i.e. divorce, new job, etc., you may find yourself right back where you were when a similar trigger or situation occurs. Understanding that you are just hallucinating that it is the same will help you get through the suffering faster and spend less time on these thoughts or emotions.

I am clear that suffering is the darkness in my life that is trying to steal my light. You don't need to believe in spiritual warfare to see we can be attacked from the inside out. Although the reason you are suffering is not life or death, your physical body takes a beating. It will help you to strive to minimize suffering in your life by thinking differently. Let's take a look at some specific areas of self-suffering and pain that are universal to many women and how we might grow through them.

Self-Pity

Self-pity is a pit of despair you can get caught in when you are overwhelmed. You usually can't tell you're stuck there until someone or something disrupts it. We may take on too many things that will cause us to eventually break if we don't take care of ourselves. When we empty ourselves of emotional and physical energy, we start feeling sorry for ourselves. We take on a "Why me?"

feeling that can spiral us into self-pity. Thoughts of blame or fantasies of being rescued are the two most common thought threads.

Blaming becomes easy when we are here. Looking at external pressure or situations as the cause of our disruption is much easier to do than acknowledging we took on too much. Whether it is your partner, kids, boss, the weather, or anything else that you choose to blame, it means your mindset is off and you need a readjustment. I know my expectations of others are way too high when I find myself here. I didn't think about how much I was taking on or the long-term impact it could have on my energy level.

Some things are out of our hands though and we didn't ask to take them on. We need to evaluate if we had strong enough boundaries or too high expectations for how we could handle them. Taking care of my dad, who often has struggled since my mom died, has triggered a lot of self-pity for me. I felt sorry for myself until I finally took the pressure off and believed that I was not responsible for his happiness. I spend a large amount of time helping him with things I wish he could do himself. I have had to adopt a new mindset that I can only do the best I can and not allow this to steal my joy. I have had so many *"why me?"* moments since my mom was diagnosed with dementia in 2001 and most of our family's burdens began to fall on my shoulders. This mindset never made it better, only worse creating a tornado that swirled with every new incident or responsibility that arose. I can also feel this way when it comes to parenting and I want more for my kids than they do.

The reality is I am competent and driven. Not everyone is like this, so I take on all the responsibility but then get angry for having taken it on. I want to change other people when this happens. I wish the people around me could sense it and do things to help while I am busy instead of just sitting there. I wish my daughter would take the initiative and get moving. I wish my son would want to study and accept responsibility. I wish my ex was better at helping the kids and holding them accountable. I wish there was someone other than me in my family who could take care of my parents.

As I allow this wave of emotions to pass, I will take a few minutes to go outside and just breathe. I know I am falling into self-pity and need to change my state. Yelling at my kids, or being angry at my ex seems like it would help, but I have the awareness to know it will only make it worse. I usually can sense that it is coming from a deep sadness that my mom is gone and I am the head of my family now. Instead, I choose acceptance and prayers. Instead of yelling, I become more patient. Instead of pushing my kids away, I pull them closer and try to be more understanding. I know my patterned history doesn't work and I suck at asking for help. I know we all deserve downtime and judging people for taking it only means I need more. I also will call my ex and tell him I am grateful for him because although he isn't the man I want to be married to I do appreciate all he does for us. He usually would sense I was in self-pity as we stood next to one another at a soccer game and I hammered him about how the kids did on homework that week.

When we feel self-pity, it is an opening for some serious self-reflection and compassion. As women and mothers, we are wired differently. We cannot expect others to be the same. We need to focus on where we can grow and love more, not what others could be doing differently. We will be alone forever if we strive to control everyone else's behavior or our environment.

It takes tremendous practice to get to the point where you don't allow triggers to affect your behavior. I am at the point where words don't come out, but I still become distant. I retreat until I can move through the emotions without blaming anyone else. Fortunately, my loved ones understand this is how I work through things and respect the space I need.

Being Stuck

Have you ever been so sad or overwhelmed that you feel like your emotions are shut off? Even though you want to get it out you can't feel anymore? You stay trapped in a place where you should be grieving or sad, but you aren't. I used to think this was a good thing. I thought I was just stronger or more resilient than others. What I have found over the years is that I will abandon my feminine essence quickly if I am facing challenges. I step into my masculine and just try to get shit done. I become robotic and detached from the problem.

This can get me through the toughest parts, but eventually I want to collapse and feel again. I want to cry and fall apart knowing that trapping my emotions inside will catch up with me sooner or later. I realize showing my feminine side didn't come naturally for me before. I have to be intentional about showing it. My mind had a super-strong protection system that I continuously rubbed up against.

You may be stuck if:
- You cannot process grief.

- You aren't grateful when you wake up or when you go to bed.
- You are overthinking your situation.
- You are stressed, anxious, or are worrying constantly.
- Your past has created emotional blocks.
- You are allowing fear to drive or paralyze you.
- You don't know who you are.
- You don't have a vision or goals.
- You feel hopeless.
- You are projecting, blaming, or displacing negativity onto others.
- You are uncertain about your purpose.
- You aren't aware how your preferences are stealing your joy.
- Your life is not aligned with your values and priorities.
- Your physical body is suffering from fatigue.

I am aware I have to make a major shift whenever I find myself thinking too much instead of feeling. It means I have to let go of control and slow down. I have to be intentional about taking some time to process what has happened. I imagine a wall around my heart and envision it coming down. I sink into the discomfort of my emotions. Usually waves of them show up: sadness, anger, anxiousness, fear, doubt, and resentment. Rather than judging myself for any of them, I let them roll past me. I feel through each one and share my gratitude that I have the ability to feel. I used to hate this and would stay in denial over them, but now I just make sure they are metabolized and not stored in my body.

I don't do this throughout the day. I set aside time when I journal to get it all out. I write on the raw intensity of whatever I am feeling. I also process some of it with my therapist, Kathi. Going through it with her allows me to give me feedback that it's okay to have all the thoughts and emotions that I do.

Kathi has become one of my greatest teachers and she helped me get unstuck. The way she came into my life was absolutely orchestrated by divine intervention. I was at an event with a close friend and we had chosen the breakout session that we wanted to attend which dealt with courage, business, and balance. Another session was being offered at the same time dealing with aging parents with Alzheimer's. I had told my friend that I was choosing to function in my high level of denial about my mother a little longer and would pass on this session. At this point in 2007, I had both my children and my mother in diapers and I hadn't fully grieved her illness yet.

As we walked to the room assigned for the session, the doors closed. We were literally two seconds late. They wouldn't let us in, no matter how much we tried. Little did I know this was the first of many *life is happening for me* moments. My friend nudged my attention to the open door to the right and said this might be a sign. It was the session on aging parents. I found myself sitting near the front row. The session was incredible with a panel of powerful women sharing not only how they handle their parent's diseases, but also how they became more authentic and clear because of them. I walked out knowing that my mom's mind dying every day was a metaphor for what I also needed to make happen within my own mind.

My friend recommended that I meet Kathi when we got home to help me start grieving knowing my mom's disease would eventually take her. Kathi was her mentor and someone she believed had reached total consciousness or wholeness. She was right. Kathi helped me create my process for thought management without even realizing it. She led me through some of my deepest fears and preferences. She was there for me while my mom was dying, my divorce, my kid's struggles, my relationship challenges, and years of ego versus love conversations. She is and was a gift from God. She helped me soften my edges and find the peace I needed to feel grateful. Kathi helped me find my Big Voice. Before I met Kathi, I hadn't realized that I was stuck and needed a teacher to help me.

When you are a perfectionist, you view being emotional as a bad thing because you feel others won't see you as strong. Your inside world doesn't match your outside world. It is okay to feel sadness, anger, frustration, or hurt. What is not okay is to project it on others or beat yourself up for it. You do not want to punish others because you can't handle your emotions. My commitment is to being loving and kind no matter what I am going through. If I am frustrated with someone, I choose to not react to them. I continue to be kind and open. I look at my frustration as something I can grow through. Perhaps I can have a rational conversation with the person to see if we could do anything differently. If I didn't allow myself to feel my frustration and just distracted myself from it, nothing would ever change.

Make a commitment to handle suffering differently so that you can live an extraordinary life and not feel stuck. Decide that it is part of your daily routine, just like the exercise you fit in your schedule. Wake up early and get all of your emotions out through journaling. At this time ask for God's guidance and support to keep you focused. Hand it over to Him rather than believing you have to do anything. Trusting in Him that life will unfold exactly as you need it to will strengthen and empower you to keep moving forward on your goals.

Lack of Balance

Women fight so hard to have the same rights and opportunities as men. We have had the right to vote less than 100 years. Maintaining healthy habits, raising a family, taking care of aging family members, doing charity work, maintaining friendships, and being a good partner or spouse all take time and energy. When you stack them on top of a career it is no wonder you feel overwhelmed. It's easy to see how the challenge with breaking the glass ceiling has caused issues with being able to balance it all.

We live on a super-woman or imbalanced, crazy woman spectrum where most of us lack balance. Learning how to prioritize conflicting responsibilities and make everyone happy can be frustrating. We often feel exhausted and guilty because we want to help, but don't ask for it easily if we ask at all.

Balance is a tough place to describe, but when I achieve it I have some common feelings. I know that I have done the best I can. I have managed my day to ensure I get some "me" time. I have eaten healthy and exercised. My kids know I love them and am not burdened by them. I feel rested. I have been present wherever I am. At work I am not focused on my kids and at home I am not focused on my work. I am not plagued with guilt and I easily let go of mistakes. I have delegated and asked for help when I need it. I have an abundance of energy.

I love being in that balanced state and unless something major has happened I can stay there 90 percent of the time. Being a career mom, I have had to give up a lot. I don't prioritize drinking or socializing. I can't stay up late. I can't be the mom that volunteers a ton at school and can only be the one who donates money or store-bought goods. If I forget to drop off something at school for a party, I quickly let it go. I am clear I am a drop-off mom and my kids don't expect me to park and walk them to class. I always joke with them that I have pre-funded a therapy account for all the things they will find one day I did wrong because I chose to work. I am okay if I only get five minutes of exercise a day or if I eat bread at lunch. In this state I have surrendered and let go of trying to control everything.

However, for the other ten percent of my time, which might be your 90 percent right now, I am completely out of balance. My brain won't shut off about work at home and when I'm at work I am researching relationship articles or thinking about my kids' schedules or struggles. I am irritable at my ex that he doesn't take more responsibility for disciplining the kids so it doesn't all fall on me. I am hopeless that I will ever get my kids off their phones and games. Although I am reviewing my goals daily, I am not taking massive action towards them. There is never enough time and I am worn out. Life continues to be a hamster wheel where every day I sacrifice my own wants and needs to serve everyone else.

None of us divide our time or priorities the same, so finding balance is an individual quest. Once you feel you have found it, something will likely change again. The speed in which people move and the quantity of activities people have in their lives is going to make feeling balanced close to impossible. Prioritizing and getting really clear on what is important will help you realign your days to carve out at least a bath or moment for you. If you are one of those women who overbook your schedule repeatedly, you might have some deeper work to do beyond simply prioritizing. If your worth and significance are tied to being a supermom, fitness freak, overachiever, or workaholic finally finding balance might feel like ending an addiction.

We can become addicted to being busy all the time. We might be using busyness to distract us from other things or because it makes us feel important, but this is a trap that will eventually burn you out. Your personality type is an important consideration when evaluating balance. If you are a procrastinator you will likely feel out of balance a lot. If you are a control freak you will likely have time management nailed down, but also feel out of balance because you lack freedom to enjoy life.

My friend, Anese Cavanaugh, an amazing speaker and writer, helped me make a major shift in how I felt just by adjusting my language. Although my life is busy rather than saying so to everyone who asked I just responded that it was full. It is crazy how this subtle shift helped me feel more powerful and clear that I am the one that has the power to either fill up or empty my schedule depending on what my life has time for.

We've never had an entire generation of working women to role model balance for us. Although progress has been made in shattering the glass ceiling and we now have much more opportunity, the quality of our lives has actually gone down. We are dealing with the shards of glass that got stuck as we were pushing through. Financially we are more independent, but emotionally we aren't juggling life as well. I believe this is because we have not stayed feminine and true to ourselves in gaining professional success. Many of us are strong alpha women, yet we still have a soft feminine side. Being out of balance forces us to stay in our masculine so we can get shit done. Staying here for long will deplete us and cause severe fatigue.

When I am using too much masculine energy I eventually break down and fall into a deep exhaustion. I can feel my adrenal system being over-taxed as basic decisions add up and I push myself too far. If I have a lot going on with my kids, work, family, or relationship my anxiety levels soar and I find myself running on adrenaline to keep it all together. My monkey-mind kicks in and I start feeling sorry for myself or hopeless that anything will ever change.

Women also experience that feeling of being out of balance when we multitask too much. We are capable of it, but it is not good for our brain or health. It is much more effective to do one thing at a time and be completely focused and present. I think we can all picture the woman in the board room with milk stains on her shirt trying to be taken seriously. It is unrealistic to think that we can be as present as we need to be if we are doing more than one thing at a time.

Achieving more balance is not hopeless, but does require energy and discipline. After you clearly define your priorities you simply must "time block" them. On Sundays, I review my week and make decisions up front about my schedule. I ensure weekly dinners at home are prepped or shopped for so I don't lose steam and end up in a drive-thru later in the week. I plan exercise days and do them whether I feel like it or not. I take time for self-care and read while taking a bath. I am in charge of my week so if something unexpected happens I have a choice to say no. If you are crystal clear on your top priorities, then you cannot take other projects or things on. If you do, you ultimately end up being mad at yourself for either flaking or having too much on your plate.

You cannot stay balanced forever. Life is ultimately outside of your control and will throw you curve balls. You need the awareness to feel it when you are out and to create a plan quickly to overcome it. You can't beat yourself up or wallow in self-pity for long.

Loneliness

Many of us have a deep sense of loneliness in our lives even when we are living our best life. Loneliness has nothing to do with being alone. It doesn't matter if you are struggling, or suffering, or feel like you have it all. The common bond we all share is a tiny ache or calling that is sometimes unquenchable.

Two people have been instrumental to me in understanding this phenomenon: Stasi Eldredge, a Christian author, and Dr. Wayne Dyer, a philosopher and self-help author. They both agree something exists deep inside that leads us closer to God and our divine purpose. Stasi in her book *"Captivating"* shares the deepest desires of every woman. She articulates so well the deep yearning of our souls to be loved, seen, and captivating. Recognizing that our human search for this can be disappointing, she suggests that God has placed this desire in us so we eventually turn to Him for all that we crave. Dr. Dyer believes in divine impersonal intelligence. He suggests when you finally understand the concept you will feel more alive and driven. In his words it is your soul's yearning for connection and if you aren't following it you will feel alone.

Loneliness has been a very common feeling for me since my life fell apart and I awakened. As I looked around at many of the people in my life, I realized I didn't have a deep and truthful connection with them. I thought at first it was because they didn't value growth the same way I did and appeared content living life the same way they always had. As I changed I felt alienated from them. I don't think a lot of people understand I didn't choose this path, but rather it chose me. What I realized over time though, was I was causing the loneliness and that my relationships with them had to change. I had to let them meet the new me, the one that admitted I had been struggling. I have since reconnected with many of the people I'd been avoiding for years because I took ownership of my loneliness. In the world of achievement you hear that proximity is power or you are only as successful as your five closest friends but this cannot apply to deep friendships you have had for a lifetime. There are people who love you unconditionally and will bring you fulfillment. Don't make the mistake I did and push them away. It will help your journey to connect with like-minded people but don't walk away from deep connections you have with others that might live differently then you.

I know I cannot go back and live the way I did before. My purpose guides me and the discipline I have brings me joy. I have a deep craving for knowledge. If I have to choose between reading and going to the bars, the choice is simple. I hate small talk now and even worse I hate the context of what most people discuss. So many women gossip or connect by complaining. Most of the men talk about sports or money and success. I try to avoid all of this and have become more selective of who I spend my time with.

I live a simple life. I love being with my kids, watching their sports, hiking, traveling, going to growth events, and occasionally socializing. Sometimes the loneliness can be uncomfortable but only when you focus on it or buy into the idea I need to be in a relationship to be happy. Recognize that if you are feeling loneliness, even with a full life, that you are changing. You are becoming your true authentic self and the internal contentment you will find when you are alone is worth this struggle.

Anxiety

Everyone has experienced anxious feelings, but how do you know if you have anxiety? What exactly is it and how does it affect your life? Anxiety is an emotion characterized by an unpleasant state of inner turmoil often accompanied by nervous behavior. It is not the same as fear, which is a response to a real or perceived threat. Anxiety is the expectation of future threat.

Men and women typically experience anxiety in different areas of their lives. Men are more anxious about their careers and finances and women about their relationships, health, and vanity. This makes it comical for us to understand one another. Men may get annoyed because we worry about things they don't. We in turn may grow frustrated as they focus more energy on work and achievement than family or health. A man's desire to provide and protect is deeply rooted in their value system just like a woman's is to nurture and look good doing it. When you look at how deep these primitive desires are you can't help laughing at how life has evolved around them. Men seem to have an unquenchable desire for more success and money and women an unquenchable thirst to look better and take care of even more people or things. The challenge is when we take it to an unhealthy level by constantly comparing ourselves to others which makes us feel we can never be enough.

For me anxiety is a state where I am contemplating things and constantly hypothesizing. I don't have moments of peace or relaxation. I am so driven to my purpose that every minute is spent finding how to live a perfect life. It takes intention for me to let go and be trusting. When I am writing, exercising, taking a bath, or finally have given myself permission to relax it goes away slightly, but never completely. I fear not doing enough or missing something so my mind wants to be active. Reading and praying are the two things I can do that completely shut off my anxious thoughts.

Having an older sister was a struggle because I was so competitive even from a young age. I wanted to be better, prettier, and favored more by my parents. I am certain this had a negative impact on my sister because her personality wasn't as dominant as mine. The more I craved attention, the more my anxiety went up. I wondered constantly about where I was on the popularity spectrum or how boys viewed me.

My anxiety heightened as I started dating. Not only did I want to be perfect, but I needed who I was dating to have the same standards. I was constantly judging their behavior like I was being measured by it. The most painful memories I have are of when my high school boyfriend embarrassed me by cheating with someone I didn't like. This triggered massive anxiety because I thought I loved him and was torn by my perceptions of what others were thinking. I believe I began to build a coat of armor around my heart to deal with the hurt I felt. I responded with retaliation because I thought it would take away my pain and pretended like I didn't care. This negative relationship lasted most of my high school and early college years. It took up so much energy in my life that I normalized it.

Because of my early relationship issues, this is still an area of my life that creates anxiety. The two-punch combo of negative values: perfectionism and fear of rejection, sometimes puts me in a state of anxiety that can throw me off. If I don't find a way to laugh at myself when I am in a relationship or dating my life gets heavy.

I have had to accept I had a fantasy of a relationship that had perfect standards for who I wanted to be and who I required him to be. This fantasy was created from both a failed marriage and a failed relationship that occurred after the marriage dissolved. I looked at all my patterns and triggers that I rubbed up against and thought I could avoid all of these things. Then as I hit the dating scene I knew my vision wasn't realistic so I began to settle. Deep down I just wanted a man I could respect and who was strong enough to handle my alpha personality but because I wanted to be loved so badly I didn't hold my standards. I now know I could have avoided this if I had created a relationship vision that was more clear and realistic. Once I had more self-awareness I made the decision to be open-hearted and allow God to guide this part of my life. I truly want God to guide me into whatever relationship He wants for me. I sincerely believe I am accepting and capable of unconditional love and I am committed to ending this suffering and staying in hope.

Our mind is guilty of creating hamster wheels or figure eights where we are stuck in endless loops that produce anxiousness. We all have areas of our life that cause us anxiety. Identifying the areas you have it most in will help you. Some people have general anxiety and worry about everything but others only worry about specific areas of their life. It is important to really look back as far as you can to see when and why this started.

We overcome anxiety and worry by recognizing it. The more aware we are the more power we have to make good decisions. We usually want to disrupt it by distracting ourselves with negative choices. We simply need to see it and know this too shall pass. The next step is reminding yourself this is a choice and thinking too much won't bring you the clarity you need. It will only cause you to imagine the worst. When I say that I have anxiety out loud and label it, it also helps.

"Who of you by worrying can add a single hour to your life?" Luke 12:25

Self-Doubt and Fear

Self-doubt can be a tricky thing that shows up in your life randomly. It is the false belief that you are not a unique masterpiece and are not deserving of an extraordinary life. It says things like: "You will never succeed at that," "Your stomach is not flat enough," "You are not a good mom." This feeling of self-doubt exists because we have allowed the thoughts and emotions our Little Voice produces to guide us.

Ironically, you can have confidence and self-doubt at the same time. Your Big Voice might guide you to step outside your comfort zone, but all the while your Little Voice is sprinkling questioning thoughts at you. Imagine you are at a job interview. You look amazing and feel prepared, yet as you are sitting and waiting, thoughts fly at you like: "What if I trip?" "What if they don't like me?" "What if he focuses on my lack of education?" "What if I have stuff on my face?" Suddenly you are nervous and worried whereas moments before you felt great about how qualified you are and how you looked.

Why does this happen? Why does self-doubt come in to make us feel weaker or smaller than we are? Why does it compare us to other women? Why does it allow us to take things personally when we know we shouldn't? Self-doubt wants so badly for us to feel sorry for ourselves. Self-doubt says: "It is so hard," "I am so lonely," "I have to understand why I am feeling this way." It wants you to believe something is wrong with ONLY YOU and that other women don't suffer with these same thoughts.

Self-doubt will try to override your confidence. It will grab onto comments or opinions others say or have about you as supporting proof. Maybe you want to be a leader and are looking to apply for a new position at your company. But years ago you mentioned your desire to lead and a coworker told you then that you didn't have the strength to hold others accountable. Your Little Voice allows this memory to suddenly creep back in and makes you question yourself.

As women, we have an internal compass that we should listen to more often. Self-doubt will try to override your intuition. It will challenge it and get you to worry more about whatever you are facing. This happens in parenting with me all the time. I know in my gut what the right decision is, but then self-doubt crops up making me worry about whether my kids will like me or if I should have handled something differently.

The worry self-doubt produces is a waste of our time. We cannot think our way into the right decision or path in life. That doesn't mean we shouldn't research things or validate them, but staying lost in a battle between your highest and lowest self will only wear you out.

Fear is just a way that self-doubt shows up. Whether we fear failure, success, or rejection it doesn't matter. Fear in any form is doubt that you deserve to live an amazing life.

I wish there were a way out of having self-doubting thoughts. I have not personally succeeded at doing this, but have used my Thought Management Strategy to not allow them to guide me or affect the way I feel. I celebrate this victory because before my self-doubting thoughts made me become passive and discontent.

We must rise above self-doubt to find our Big Voice. There is absolutely no reason why we cannot allow our strength and confidence to drive us and quit having internal conflict. You have to believe me that you are exactly where you are supposed to be without regret, shame, or guilt from your past or anxiety or worry about your future. All of the self-doubt and fear you have is only designed to keep you in suffering and no longer serves you.

Shame and Guilt

I wish we all knew early on how these two emotions appeared in our life. They are devastating to us both internally and externally. As you learned earlier your brain rewards you with "feel good" hormones for experiencing shame and guilt. They keep you from being your highest self. They keep you stuck in patterned thinking where your Little Voice is in control; protecting you from more perceived hurt.

We typically do one of two things when we carry shame and guilt. We punish ourselves or we punish everyone around us. When we punish ourselves, we stay small and passive. Fear and regret are our guiding values. We don't truly accept that we can be forgiven and restored. The heaviness of these emotions can show up in many different ways. We might stay in a relationship that is harmful to us emotionally or physically. We might not take care of our bodies to protect us from intimacy or attention. We might be addicted to drugs or alcohol. We might be addicted to gossip or judgment. We might be the consummate helper trying to appear happy. We might feel we are getting what we deserve.

When we are in this state, our ego can try and stop us from being grateful or capable of prioritizing love. We aren't really living; we are simply existing. We might have moments of happiness or fun but these emotions don't sustain us especially when we are alone with our thoughts. It doesn't matter where the shame and guilt actually come from. They have the effect of stealing our confidence and faith.

We are less likely to be a spiritually successful woman if we are plagued by our past. For most of us, we have the intention of letting go but life goes by too fast. If we don't deal with shame and guilt on a daily basis but continue thinking about it the pain will get worse. Trying to avoid thoughts of them doesn't work. If you fall into this category you must focus on forgiveness and self-love. It is important that you make the decision to become authentic but you can't be authentic if you are carrying burdens from your past.

You should understand you will continue to make mistakes generating more stuff to feel guilty and ashamed about. Layering on more guilt and shame will make you both physically and emotionally sick. Your body is not built for the amount of emotional stress you put on yourself. Learning how to quickly move on will help you going forward. Imagine a day that you simply let it all go and fully accept your humanness. Life will fall into place for you then and you will have the confidence to do anything you desire.

Instead of torturing ourselves, sometimes guilt and shame can cause us to torture those around us. Our children or partners are usually the primary victims but the torture can spread to anyone in our life. Projection is one of the most basic human defenses. Instead of fully feeling your own emotions you project your shame and guilt on others.

These feelings often show up as controlling behavior. Your Little Voice wants to protect you so much it builds a wall around your heart. We all have a preferred method of projection. Like self-sabotage if we spend time getting curious about how we project our emotions onto others we can set our intentions to avoid doing it. The reason we do it is simple. It is far easier for our brain to avoid these powerful emotions by putting them onto others. We see other people projecting every day. Someone has a fight with their spouse and attacks a coworker because of a mistake. Someone is afraid their kids will encounter the same negative situation they did as a child so they become a helicopter mom and try to control everything.

My preferred method of dealing with shame and guilt has been to push people away. If I feel these emotions it's like I want to hurt myself more because deep down I don't think I deserve love or joy. I pick others apart for a myriad of reasons and focus on things that don't really matter. Until I wake up and realize what I am doing, I am convinced that it is the other person who is wrong. I tend to project more feelings of shame and guilt when I am hormonal. It is easier to blame others than to deal with my own growth opportunities. I have to be completely aware of where I am in my cycle and track my emotions in my journal. Overnight I can go from feeling blessed to being intolerable of someone else's imperfections or choices.

Projecting

Our projections can hurt other people deeply. We tend to withhold love and are not as trusting of God's plans. In reality, we hurt ourselves the most. Every moment we get angry and lash out is just another reason to beat ourselves up later. Every time we blame someone else we miss an opportunity to grow. Every time we withhold love, we miss out on love and joy ourselves. Every time we think we can control life we miss out on precious present moments. Projecting delays our own inner journey. Getting a handle on it will free you to fully let go of what you have been carrying and be so much lighter.

Beyond shame and guilt, we often project our

fears onto others. Usually fear is linked to shame and self-doubt in some way. Maybe you were in a relationship where someone cheated. You are ashamed you had no idea what was going on and feel embarrassed you were that stupid. You haven't let go of the feeling and every time you get into a relationship you are guarded so that it doesn't happen again. You glance at his text messages, want to know where he is at all times, and try to control him. Your fears are being projected onto an innocent person. All you need is awareness and honesty of this to get through it. Hiding your shame or fears will only make it worse.

Be aware that even after you move through them and feel restored, they may continue to pop up. These thoughts are intruders and you cannot let them guide you. The memories are forever stored deep in you so your new mindset must be stronger than they are. You can pray that one day they will stop following you but there is no guarantee. I use these thoughts in my life now to celebrate how far I have come. My "lower self" made a lot of stupid decisions before I was awake, some of them hurting others deeply. Although I have forgiven myself, occasionally something triggers these shameful emotions or thoughts to arise. As I sit and let them pass I say, "I am restored and celebrate that the person I am today would not make these mistakes. I am released from any guilt or shame."

Life is about failing and making mistakes. We cannot possibly live a perfect life. God doesn't want us to be punished forever. Accept that your brain is rogue and laugh at it. When these thoughts and feelings make themselves known again, giggle and say, "Really? Why now? These old things can no longer scare me or make me feel anything other than the masterpiece I know I am."

"God's perfect love drives out fear." Psalm 34:4

Body Image and Health Issues

Many women seek having the perfect body or are in a constant state of trying to change their body. Magazines showcase women who look to be flawless. We know logically that they are air-brushed and spend a lifetime trying to look that way. Not a day goes by that you don't encounter a woman complaining about her body or dieting to try and do something about it (or change it). The comparisons we make and discontentment we feel physically can affect every other aspect of our life.

We have an obsessive brain that delights in producing thoughts and emotions that align with our Little Voice's thoughts *unless* we feed it a new pattern. We have all watched an eating disorder take someone's joy or their life. We have watched someone's desire to control a situation manifest into their relationship with food. It can devastate you if you don't feel amazing about your body.

Our physical health must be a top priority, but not because of how we look. Vanity doesn't matter in the end. For those of you who believe in God we will one day leave this body behind and join Him in heaven. I always imagine my first conversation with Him as a funny hallucination where He says, "I am disappointed you never got those buns of steel you focused on so much. What is wrong with you? Why didn't you do squats more?" See how silly that is? I have found a way to prioritize health but it is not about getting an hour in at the gym every day. It is about doing random things throughout the day like pushups on my kitchen counter while I am cooking or squats when I am blow drying my hair. Just make a commitment to move more and your health will improve.

It is true that life is easier when you take care of your body and do not use food to manage your emotions. I read a quote that said, "Don't let what's on the outside distract someone from finding out what is on the inside." It is not worth it to use our physical bodies to carry shame and guilt and to give ourselves all the negative aspects of obesity like diabetes, fatigue, sleep apnea, or low confidence.

We have to become aware and realize the world wants us unhappy. When we are unhappy we spend more money on food, alcohol, medication, healthcare, and diet systems or fads. There is a lot of money to be made when we are suffering.

Businesses see your obsession with weight management and have made billions from slimming clothes (the founder of Spanx is worth over 1 billion according to Forbes) to pharmaceuticals to gym memberships you don't use. We all crave the quick fix. We want to look and feel better yet get stuck in the same patterned thinking day after day. Most women start a diet, then they exercise, then they feel restrained and splurge for a weekend, then they beat themselves up for splurging, then they start over again. It is an endless cycle. Monday's seem to be the day we choose to start over every week.

We are too smart to allow ourselves to fall victim to societal bias and marketing. It's only how we feel that matters. We need to realize the food industry exploits our suffering and uses our need to feel good against us. Food can be a powerful drug and can be addicting. Your body works better when you are fueling it with non-processed, chemical-free, inflammatory reducing, natural foods. When I made the decision to only eat organic food and cut out sugar my physical and mental health improved significantly.

For me, the best way to approach this area was to admit body or self-obsession was an addiction. Looking in the mirror as a barometer for self-confidence or feeling bad about our bodies is ludicrous. Comparing ourselves to one another is a waste of time. Make the decision to get healthy and drop vanity going forward. We need to step into our most powerful selves so we can use our strength to change the world. The only way to do this is by prioritizing health and healing over our physical appearance.

Creating a movement where more women love themselves fully requires support from all women. Anyone that obsesses over their physical appearance is suffering. For starters, the skinny people need to quit saying they are fat and the obese people need to quit pretending they don't care. You have to find a healthy place in the middle where you feel vibrant and energetic; where your physical and emotional health is your top priority.

I imagine a world where our only measurement is how we feel. Do we have energy and vitality? Not what dress size am I or how do others see me. Health is not a competition. We shouldn't take care of our bodies because it matters to the opposite sex. Let it go. Trust me that a strong body will come if you don't obsess about the one you have and make small steps every day towards getting healthy.

Acting Strong and Perfectionism

The energy it takes trying to appear strong and in control is more than we can generate. When we store up our pain and suffering, run from our problems, and appear on the outside we have it all together, we are stunting our growth and ability to be present. Caring more about what others think than how you feel yourself is called perfectionism.

If you look back on your childhood when times were tough or you faced making a decision it is likely that you didn't get the wisdom or tools you could use as an adult. Parents often came to our rescue to shield us or got angry and enforced consequences. Some were indifferent, leaving us to feel like they didn't care. Occasionally there were those rare intentional parents who gave their children timeless lessons.

Now as we deal with adult-sized problems our pre-patterned defense system kicks in automatically. Accepting this system is faulty and will lead to even more suffering is critical. When we use our energy trying to act strong or distract ourselves rather than dealing with the real situation or problem, it catches up with us. We may break emotionally or physically, but we will break. Life will eventually lead you to deal with it once and for all.

I see this happen often in shaky marriages. Rather than dealing with things daily, women can live for years unhappy or angry, in silence, thinking they are being strong for the sake of their children. The more we fail to communicate what we are feeling, the worse it will get. If we are fearful of speaking up because we feel we can't risk it, it becomes more painful. Feeling trapped, believing you need to feel perfect, steals your joy.

After I read *Power of Now* by Eckhart Tolle, I finally started to awaken to the fact that I was just acting strong and didn't really feel that way internally. I had been living on auto-pilot for so long and was miserable. I was exhausted. I felt like on a scale of 1 to 10 with one being unconscious and ten being awake, I was a 1. I began to watch my thoughts and emotions and was able to stop them from affecting my actions. The unintended consequence was that I also stopped listening to my Big Voice thoughts as well. This left me with an emptiness I had not experienced before because

I became extremely passive which was not in alignment with my personality. I believe I needed to go through this to understand that waking up on your own without guidance or a teacher is harder to do. I found I could be strong and still seek help from others. It humbled me to realize that I couldn't face this journey alone.

It is imperative to be honest with yourself when you aren't feeling confident and strong. You can become more powerful if you are more vulnerable. That may seem impossible, but it is okay to feel raw and real when you struggle. The important thing is to find a support network.

Experiencing Joy and Suffering Simultaneously

In the Bible, Paul tells us that we can expect suffering on earth and to find a way to rejoice in it. According to Isaiah, 53:10-11, God wanted His son Jesus to suffer so that all of us could be saved. I believe God knows we will suffer in this broken world, but will be there for us whenever we turn to Him. He will use our suffering to teach us lessons we couldn't have learned otherwise. The Bible goes on in Isaiah to say that after Jesus suffers he will see the light of life. The message is that one day in heaven we will live a perfect life where there will be *"no more death or mourning or crying or pain, for the old order of things has passed away."* (Revelation 21:1:4) Whether you are a believer or not, we can all learn lessons from the bible and how we can accept suffering as a part of our life.

Can we find a way to rejoice in suffering? We absolutely can if we change our perspective and mindset. The secret is to letting go and letting God handle our futures or problems and to continue to cultivate joy in spite of our circumstances. Realize the suffering you are experiencing is an unwanted visitor and will leave at some point. The more you think of it as bad, the worse it becomes. Kathi, my spiritual warrior and therapist, shared a simple analogy with me that resonates when I am suffering. She described suffering as an annoying aunt that just stopped by for an unannounced visit. You don't know how long she will stay. You know you have better or more productive ways you could use your time, but for right now she is there. Sitting with the discomfort of visiting with her is necessary. She won't leave and you might as well make the best of it.

If you look at suffering as an opportunity to remain in your Big Voice in spite of your preferences for your life not being met, you can stay in joy. You can celebrate that you were present and actively listening to life's experiences speaking to you. You can celebrate that you were trying to find wisdom in whatever the situation is.

We want suffering to end and we try our hardest to make that happen. If we asked our aunt to leave immediately we would face even more suffering because chances are we would beat ourselves up for being a bad person or when the rest of our family called us rude. We have to change from the inside out to fully accept that suffering is simply a part of life. We have to end pushing people away when suffering happens and distracting ourselves with nonsense.

The only way to find more peace and lasting joy is through awareness and self-love. Accept that you make it worse when you think you have to do something about it. You need to be patient and curious. You need to take inventory of where your Little Voice is trying to lead you and why. I find giving and serving others at times I am suffering helps me get through those seasons faster. When I was only a month into my sister's situation and suffering tremendously with anxiety and grief, my kids and I went on a mission trip and helped a ton of kids that were less fortunate. I know we made a difference in their lives and it helped me personally through the worst season I have ever been in.

It is important to remember that as humans it

would be impossible to be filled with joy and gratitude all the time. We are not immune to life's challenges so we should expect there are things in the world that will make us sad, angry, or triggered. We also have a need for variety and uncertainty. What this means is we will often disrupt our own lives out of sheer boredom without even realizing it. We cannot be "Stepford" women where everything is rosy and balanced all the time.

To offset the boredom you feel you can create a vision or set of goals that is a stretch from where you are. Having a desire that is outside your comfort zone, exciting, or stimulating will feed your desire for variety. Most women get so accustomed to taking care of others they don't set their own goals. If you want to suffer less and experience more joy, you must start feeding your needs or your subconscious mind will do it for you.

You can cultivate a source of sustainable joy. As you look around at friends, family, or strangers far too many people aren't present and filled with joy. Life is always going to present issues to complain about, but try to find a well of joy deep within that can overcome any struggle you face.

The egoless path that will set you free starts with being aware of what your Little Voice or ego sounds like. It is important that you understand how it shows up both internally and externally. It doesn't like it when external comments or situations hurt you. It will attempt to offset them with defensive thoughts or emotions to fight against whatever happened. It appears to make positive thoughts, yet will also blame the person or situation that offended or hurt you. Internally, it will stop you from speaking up, taking action, or growing through whatever you are facing. It is designed to keep you separate from others and small.

An egoless path means we don't personalize anything anyone says or does to us. It accepts that not everyone will like us or what we stand for. It is strong and mighty. It won't allow you to store anything emotionally because it knows that is what quiets our Big Voice.

An egoless path is really the only way to let go of everything you have acquired along your journey; all the accidental fear, shame, guilt, and passivity that you were never intended to hold. Letting go is really the only choice you have to live a joyful life. Suffering cannot be avoided, but can be done in a way that you remain hopeful and blessed. If we choose anger, blame or frustration we cannot be grateful at the same time.

Your next step is to get free of ego. This doesn't

mean your ego goes away, only that it will no longer drive your actions or emotions long-term. Your ego does not want what is best for you and is not seeking inner peace or joy. You must adopt unconditional love for it to avoid internal conflict. Accepting it, but not allowing it to guide your feelings long-term, will make life more peaceful. I tried to slay the sucker for years until I realized all that force and energy I was putting in was unnecessary. Making this choice will take fierce commitment to understanding ego more so you can defend against it. Finding your true authentic self, free of ego will take time.

Living an egoless life is going to take commitment. It is much easier to allow it to control and guide you and cause you suffering. Every day you are committed to this path frees you from suffering and brings you closer to sustainable joy.

Sustainable joy is constant. It is a state that no matter where you are or what has happened to you, you can find gratitude and optimism. Your situation may be overwhelming or you are struggling but you still feel connected to the idea that everything will work out and your life will be guided. Joy is different than happiness. Happiness comes in bursts. Joy fills you up like a continuous source of blessings you can tap at any time. Joy runs deep in your heart and accepts you are connected to a larger purpose. Although pleasure or meeting your worldly desires brings short-term happiness, there is nothing sustainable about it. For example, take eating chocolate. When you crave it and then eat it you get a burst of happiness or pleasure, but minutes, hours, or days later you can't pull sustainable joy from that experience. Joy is a state of well-being. It represents inner peace where no matter what, you know God is there celebrating the masterpiece you are.

Understanding that self-suffering is just a string of emotions or thoughts brought on by your Little Voice is a start. Seeing the repetitiveness of them will give you the awareness needed to remember they are only ego talking. By using the TMS strategy you will find it easier to notice when you are attacking yourself from the inside out.

Much of your self-suffering is preventable and within your power to overcome. You can stand up to these unwanted guests or impostor thoughts and not let them guide your life or steal your joy. It is time to end your own suffering. Choose to rise above it. Choose to live your best life and experience true joy like you never have before. Making this decision will bring peace and harmony into your life and onto others around you. With more women finding joy and maintaining it in the midst of suffering we will rise up to make the world a more compassionate and peaceful place.

My favorite way of explaining joy was proposed by the Dalia Lama and Archbishop Tutu. They sum it up as being untethered by the memories of the past and not bored by the anticipatory worry about the future. Strive for that every day and you will stay in your Big Voice.

"Joy is what happens to us when we allow ourselves to recognize how good things really are."
Marianne Williamson

WRITING YOUR NEW STORY

"One must always be prepared for riotous and endless waves of transformation." Elizabeth Gilbert

After you have learned how you can experience joy and suffering simultaneously, how can you shift your mindset and write a new story? You have the power to do it at any time you decide. You can change both your internal and external worlds when you make that commitment. Fear is usually what keeps you stuck and then your obsessive thoughts drive it deeper. I hope by now you have chosen to abandon fear and follow your Big Voice.

If you were to write a story about your life now, what would you say? Maybe you appear on the outside to be put together, but every night you drink three glasses of wine just to distract yourself from the pain in your marriage. Maybe you are a good mom but beat yourself up that your kids aren't grateful. Maybe you suffer from headaches every day and feel like giving up, but everyone thinks you are happy. Here is what I would like you to do. In the paragraphs below is an example of a fictional person's story. I'd like you to write your story in a similar manner. But rather than work on changing anything right away, I want you to sit with the idea that this story will never change. Seriously imagine what it would feel like if you never rise up and start living your best life.

Julie's story:

Julie is to everyone else a rock. She is always there to offer emotional support whenever anyone needs her. She is married with two kids and lives in a sleepy suburb of Los Angeles. Every day she wakes up and makes sure her family is taken care of; lunches, permission slips, grocery store visits, etc. are her priorities. After the struggle of getting the kids out the door she feels exhausted. She feels empty and confused. She thinks there has to be more to life than emptying herself every day. As she finally gets back home from drop-off, she has every intention of crossing off items on her "to do" list, but when she sits down she collapses. Her mind is filled with obsessive thoughts about her future.

Although she has been married for 15 years she feels like she can't manage another day with him. He snores, he doesn't take care of himself, he just exists, and then he wants sex twice a month. He is a good dad, but only helps when he is told what to do. He is a good provider and to the outside world a happy guy. She doesn't know what would happen if she left. She wonders if therapy would help or if this is hopeless. She wonders if it is her fault that it is so bad. She can't recall the last time she was flirty with him or was attracted to him. She wonders if it stopped when the kids arrived. She remembers pouring everything into them and rejecting her husband's affection or attention. Did he stop taking care of himself because he thought it was pointless?

She looks at the clock and it's almost time for pick-up. Did she fall sleep? How could she have not started laundry? What is for dinner? As she drives to school, her friend calls and asks if she can grab her kids too and bring them to practice. Of course she can, because her friend has a yoga class she wants to attend. Her friend looks so full of energy every time Julie sees her. She is now pissed at herself; pissed that she is the one picking up all the kids instead of being the one taking care of her. On the drive her mind is racing. *Why can't I be happy and grateful? Why can't I go back to work and be seen again? Why can't my husband look at me like he is captivated? Is this really all life is about?*

As she pulls into the circle, she sees her kids are arguing. She is literally about to lose it while she is driving away then remembers her friend's kids. How could she have forgotten them? She swings back in and with a warm smile she greets them and asks about their day. To anyone else looking in, it would appear that she cares.

During practice she races to the store to figure out dinner. Earlier in the week she had a goal to cook healthier, but now she is in line picking up already prepared and processed crap again. She thinks, *what is wrong with me? All you need to do is cook a healthy meal.* Then another voice chimes in, *why can't you pull this together?* Then one more voice chimes in quieting her down saying, *it's no big deal. They won't die from this. So what if your son is a little chubby . . . he will grow into it.* The thoughts in her head consume her and she wonders if anyone else is aware she is about to crack.

Standing at the checkout she hears her name, "Julie, It's me, Sue. I've been trying to get your attention for at least five minutes. How are you? How are the kids?" Then before she can answer, Sue goes into a 15 minute rant about the PTA and how we must do something about school lunches before she changes subjects and tells her how annoying things are with her husband. Now that they started working out he has become obsessed with getting a six-pack. Sue's voice alone is killing her and she can't wait to escape. Sue finally stops talking about herself, gives Julie a squeeze and asks, "How are you, Julie?"

Ready to answer with her standard, "Great . . . the kids are good . . . work is stressful for Bob, but it is nothing we can't handle," response, her voice cracks and tears burst out of her eyes. Rather than dealing with this inside the supermarket, she quickly excuses herself telling Sue she is hormonal and not feeling well. She mumbles to Sue as she's leaving how she was going to make chicken marsala, but seeing how she wasn't feeling well, she opted for the rotisserie chicken and already prepared sides.

When she finally gets to her car, she can't breathe. *What the hell is wrong with me? Why can't I just get through the day? Why did I have to run into Sue whose kids are perfect and whose husband looks at her like she is a model?* The Little Voice comes back: *Maybe it's just your hormones. You'll be fine tomorrow. Just go home and start over.* Then another voice: *You only have one life. You can't live this way any longer. You must find yourself! You must talk to your husband about how you are feeling. You need to get healthy physically and mentally.*

Once she is home and settled, she pours herself a fat glass of wine. She thinks to herself: *Just one. It's been a stressful day.* She gets through helping the kids with homework while getting the dinner she bought together. Just as she is beginning to relax she hears the garage door open. Her heart sinks and she dreads another night of forced conversation. She thinks: *How long has it been this way?* Counting back in her head, it must be about five years. He walks in throwing his stuff down and greets the kids warmly. They do love him, but of course they have no idea that he does nothing to help her.

After dinner, she pours herself another glass of wine and exchanges her typical banter of texts with her best friend, Kara. They both hate their husbands and share all the annoying things they do to provide some comic relief during their evening routines. Kara shares Jim couldn't find the remote, causing panic, but then her three year old found it buried under his beer belly. Julie texts Bob walked in and seduced her before dinner because he had been thinking about her all day, but then followed it up with, "Sorry. That was a daydream I had when I fell asleep listening to him updating me on his day."

As the day ends her kids argue, the dog pees on the sofa, Bob falls asleep on the couch snoring, she remembers she has snack the next day and whips up something fast. She is three glasses in as her head hits the pillow. But rather than sleep, her mind races about everything imaginable. She gets anxiety worrying about the kids in school, she worries about Bob losing his job, and she wonders how she can keep living this way. She dreams about her old job and how amazing she felt connecting with people that went deeper than small talk. She dreams about a relationship where someone cherishes her. Then a little voice calms her overthinking and says: *You can do this. You should be grateful for Bob. He is a good provider and it would be hard to make it on your own. You'll be okay...just a little more time and the kids will be old enough that you can start focusing on you.* She drifts off to sleep but thinks she hears a Bigger Voice cheering for her to "wake up" from her suffering, but she can't be sure. She will just start over tomorrow.

You may connect with one or more of the themes in Julie's story as you read it. The sacrificial aspect of her life, the acceptance of a mediocre relationship, the facade she puts up for others, the dual-thinking that goes on in her head, the distraction that wine and complaining to her friend provides. Maybe it's the anxiety and fear that keeps her paralyzed or the amount of time she has accepted living like this.

We all have a story . . . whether you are single, married, a mom, stay at home, work, do charity work or not, we have all became complacent in some area of our life and want more. We have to believe we can have it all and that it is possible!

When you re-read your own life story, look for any situations where you have settled or feel "off." You can write a new story around your new awareness. So many people, whether 30, 40, 50, or really any age, have reinvented themselves. They have abandoned fear and certainty and leaped into the unknown. You don't have to quit your job, end your marriage, or make any other big changes to write a new story. You have the power to change any situation or relationship you are in right now. Begin with changing your mindset, adopting new beliefs, re-prioritizing what is important, loving and forgiving both yourself and others, and making a decision life is too short to waste time suffering.

In my marriage, we tried for eight years to turn things around. We were both committed to trying, but just couldn't get the deeper connection I was craving. It hurt so bad to see our marriage was mediocre, especially when I was speaking to others about living an extraordinary life. Being stubborn and wanting to keep my family together,

I tried so much to change and accept him for who he was. What I didn't realize at the time was I had a hardwired recipe for respect in a relationship that was impossible for our marriage. He looked to me to be the decision maker and probably felt he was powerless. Had he exerted more power and told me he would support our family, but our lifestyle would have to change, things may have turned out differently. Honestly I don't believe I was ready to let go of control and probably made things impossible for him. At the time, I wanted him to figure out what I needed without having to tell him. In his defense I didn't really know myself, what I deeply needed or wanted in a relationship until I went through two others that failed for similar reasons. I have the awareness now to know I have no one to blame but myself for all of these ending.

The new story that I wrote fully accepts who I am, my preferences and priorities, and sees self-suffering as preventable because I choose what I do and who I do it with. It doesn't mean I don't stumble and find myself back in self-suffering because I put too much on my plate or choose to be around people who trigger me. My children are the only ones at this time that I feel I must accept completely. It's okay for me to love others and be non-judgmental, but choose not to have them in my life.

To change your story you need to start with space. You cannot expect to change your life without investing time in it. Take a day, a week, or a month to really focus on you and get curious about what is driving your internal suffering. Hire a caretaker for a month, book a spa weekend, or spend a few hours in nature. No matter your financial situation, you can find a way to escape. I crack up when I see celebrities hospitalized by exhaustion . . . I think how many of us probably feel like we should be. You must prioritize your emotional and physical well-being or you are putting your mental health at risk. It is better to deal with this now before you waste another day of your life.

Start with the decision to write a new story, then your plan will begin to unfold. Use the tools that are found in the Big Voices strategies chapter of this book to create a vision, goals, and plan. Then start spending more time on your priorities. Time will slip by so fast if you don't start now. You'll quickly find the areas you want to learn about and grow in. Perhaps your life is extraordinary already but you need to learn how to be more grateful. Or everything would be good if you had a career that fed your purpose. You may have a desire to run away because you realize you want to change everything. I can tell you that doing so would only avoid the discomfort that is necessary for you to learn.

So how does Julie start over and write her story differently? She could wait until her husband has an affair because he feels useless to her and disrespected or until a health scare wakes her up. Or ideally she could start right after drop-off because she knows in her heart she can't live another day with things unchanged. Most people wait until they "have to" versus when they believe they "need to." Imagine Julie does make the decision after drop-off and finds herself in the personal development section at the book store. She chooses a book called, *The Gifts of Imperfection* by Brené Brown, because she is beating herself up every day for not being perfect. She then finds a therapist that she can see to help her through her thoughts and emotions. Over the next year, Julie wakes up early and spends some time alone on her growth plan. She takes girls nights and weekends again and even goes on her first vacation with her husband. She starts taking classes and will become an RN by the time her kids reach junior high. Let's see how her new story turns out.

Julie wakes up early and sneaks a wondrous cup of coffee while enjoying some LA sunshine. She thinks about how much has changed in the last year and is so grateful. She reads her morning devotional and reviews her goals. As she is about to go inside, her husband wraps his arms around her. He hugs her deeply and whispers in her ear, "I cannot wait to get your hot sexy body near mine this weekend." An electric volt fires through her body and immediately she feels extreme joy. They have been connecting more since she told him the truth about how she was feeling. They embarked together on a journey of self-discovery. They are going away once a month for at least one night. She is the leanest she has ever been and has more energy.

Although it was a rocky start and there were times she didn't know if they would make it, the truth really set them free. She had confessed her insecurities and desire to have her own life. He supported her going back to school and getting a nanny to do pick-up. They talk every night now and share their deepest fears. She learned her husband was also miserable, but felt powerless and undervalued. He was using work as his escape because he didn't know where to start. He felt like nothing he did would ever be enough for her. By her pouring more into him he also had more passion and energy. She became more grateful for his hard work. They also started going to church as a family and serving others at a shelter.

Their life over a one year span had gone from being self-focused to purpose-driven.

After dropping the kids off at school she got in a great workout and met a like-minded friend for coffee. They didn't sit around complaining about their husbands or kids' schedules, but rather discussed their personal journeys. Julie listened and learned from her friend's wisdom, coming away with more awareness and self-acceptance. For the longest time she thought she was the only one suffering internally; that she was the only one with a never ending internal dialogue that wore her out on most days. After coffee, she went off to class. She had started this journey to become an RN before she had kids and was excited to go back. She wanted to make a difference in her patient's lives and show her kids that you should never give up on your dreams. As the sun heated her face, waves of joy and confidence filled her, something that was happening more and more often since she had created her life vision.

It wasn't easy writing a new story. Facing the truth that she was to blame for her own suffering rather than her husband, children, and mindset took courage. After she made the decision she couldn't do it another day, things fell into place. She knew her perfectionism, passivity, and pro-crastination needed to be tackled. She knew she didn't have any personal goals to strive for. She knew she had to be honest with her husband about her unhappiness and insecurities. Once she crafted her plan, she attacked it fearlessly. Every day became a new adventure. She joined a Bible study, met with a therapist, and read books and stories about other women who had also gone through an awakening.

God kept sending her exactly what was needed. A new friend would pop up. A brochure for a nursing program would catch her eye. As she became free of constant worry and more present, life unfolded how she needed it to.

The difference in the two stories is that it's not about overhauling your external world completely, just your internal one. Julie's story could have been that she worked full-time with no kids, was obsessed with fitness, or any other story line you could devise. What is important is that she changed how she viewed her life and started reaching for her goals.

Long-term, as you continue to move toward the amazing individual you were born to be, you may find that you do need to quit your job, move, get a divorce, or make some other major change. For right now, it's enough to change your mindset and state. I understand you may feel trapped but I ask you to make a decision to change something, no matter how small. You will start to feel better.

Creating a New Identity

Like Julie, you may have hit a point in your life where you realize you can't continue to live the way you are. Maybe from the outside you look like you have it together, but inside you're in turmoil. Your mind has spun itself into worry, anxiety, fear, shame, sadness, or some other negative emotion. You find yourself with little or no gratitude and realize your Little Voice has likely been guiding you. You may have been obsessing about one thing or another like finding a partner, ending a relationship, your body, your job, or your family. If your problems or to do list is the first thing you think of when you wake up and the last thing when you go to bed your mind is in control. Your Big Voice and its beliefs have lost power. It is easy for this to happen when you aren't living a balanced life where your top priorities are your emotional and physical health. It can also happen if you are under major stress due to external problems. We can try and prepare ourselves, but then end up losing the battle. The deeper the pathway that is tied to the experience the more work it will take to overcome.

Where do you have the greatest risks for this to

happen? Identify the areas of your life you are most vulnerable. For example, if you have always been insecure in relationships or you are in constant worry that you are in the right one, you can build your growth plan around trying to overcome this. Overcoming doesn't mean the thoughts and emotions go away, but you use your new found TMS strategies to not let them affect you. Fully assessing repetitive patterns and identifying how they have sabotaged you in the past is only part of the solution. You also have to recognize even if you are prepared and aware of what's going on you are human and may lose the battle temporarily. Beating yourself up or thinking something is wrong with you, or your thinking, only makes it worse. Therefore, you'll need a plan if you end up in turmoil. So where do you start if you want to make a decision to stop your mind from taking control resulting in a season of suffering?

You start with acceptance and surrender. You accept that your mind and its pathways have been created by your past. If you obsessed over something before, you are likely to do it again if faced with a similar situation. Accept that if you don't learn how to think differently nothing will ever change. You may have slight variations in your suffering, but it's still possible to see the patterns.

Accept and commit to disrupting your thinking; a decision that comes with discipline and strategy. You have to be willing to create plans and be honest with others around you. You will need to be open and willing to get help and feedback. Accept that if your mind does take over you will just keep trying. There is nothing wrong with you. You must be humble when this happens and try and learn from it.

You must surrender that trying too much or being attached to an outcome will only make your suffering worse. Surrender to the power your mind has had over you and all the pain it has caused you. In finding self-love and forgiveness you must be willing to forgive your mind as well. Surrender to the idea that your life is guided and if your mind does take over, it is only to help you become stronger in the future.

Be willing to start over every day, even if you feel trapped by your mind repeatedly. It is a major victory when you are aware your mind is winning. Set your intentions every night that you will arise feeling blessed in spite of whatever problem you are facing.

"If you don't design your own life plan, chances are you'll fall into someone else's plan. Guess what they have planned for you? Not much." Jim Rohn

Finding your Starting Point

I understand that some of you don't know where to start. You have been living this way for so long and do have a lot to be grateful for but you still feel like something is missing. What happens if you have zero idea what you should be doing with your life? Maybe you have a successful job, but feel a calling to make a bigger impact, or you hate your job, but have no idea what you would do otherwise. We are all faced with identity crises throughout our life. It is not just mid-life crises anymore. When we focus on personal growth and purpose it naturally leads us to wonder if there is more for us.

Fear often is what paralyzes us and keeps us from finding our truth; fear that we shouldn't be discontent or we may lose what we have if we do anything different. We want to be responsible and have a sure thing before we walk away from our current situation. We don't want to fail or lose anything. Having that mindset means you don't trust your intuition or God (Universe) to guide and provide for you. Life is so short that if you have a deep knowing something is not right; you must invest time and energy into figuring it out. Your body is a great barometer if you listen to it.

Some people have callings where they feel they are told exactly what to do. Jackie, a friend at Epic

Missions, has a story I believe most of us crave. She felt God speak to her directly about starting Epic Mission. Although it took years to break through, her vision came to life in spite of the questions of how and why. It was a miraculous story where her unshakeable faith was pushed to the edge, but then all their needs were met. You could see love and light beaming out of her and her husband even though they had let go of everything material they owned and walked away from their careers to make the vision happen.

In my life, I have gone "all in" professionally once. I walked away from a thriving mortgage business where I had control of my success. I had freedom and a team that supported me. It was easy and turnkey. I took a risk in joining a company that wanted to grow their executive team and transition their company culture. I left certainty and safety for adventure and risk. My success was now based on other people's success. It was a huge step backward financially, but it put me in a position where I could do more of what I loved, which was impacting people's joy and success with my coaching systems. I had to stretch and learn how to balance more responsibilities than I had in my old job. In essence I had to start over from being in a place of mastery. The first six years of building the platform were fun and I loved my job. Over time the business did so well that my income was back to where it had been. Once again, I grew bored. I knew there was more for me to do. Fortunately, I had learned to be patient and not rely on my own decision making. Instead of leaving my job this time, I found a way to find more passion outside of work by increasing the time I spent writing and speaking.

Another challenge we often face is wanting love so much that we sacrifice our vision or standards within relationships. We start making exceptions and believe we can change others which creates our own suffering. We then beat ourselves up when triggered by things we should have known would eventually show up again. We will continue to do this until finally we get that it's okay to have preferences and needs we cannot change. Our story cannot be about settling . . . we can demand more of life when we are truly clear about what we want.

You might start trying to change so much that you begin making choices that are far beyond what you can handle. After you awaken and have awareness, you will go through a season where you have no idea what you want or who you are. It may take a while to really see God's plan for you. You need to remain patient and trusting things will unfold for you and know you don't have to make rash decisions that could hurt others unintentionally.

Choosing Faith over Fear

"Lord, what do I wait for? My hope is in you."
Psalm 39:7

I believe in God and Jesus Christ. I was saved from my own pain and suffering when I finally surrendered my free will and earthly desires to him. I have also learned much through the teachings of Buddha, the Dalai Lama, Eckhart Tolle, Pema Chödrön, and many other religious teachers.

Although I am personally confident that my creator sent His son so that my sins would be forgiven, you don't have to be. Many of the teachings or Bible verses are universal to any faith. Life is easier if you believe in a higher power though and accept there is a universal force that is guiding us. I do not believe my life is so blessed because I am free of problems. Trust me I have had my share. I believe I have grown stronger because I had them and therefore I am more blessed. I choose simply to find opportunities for growth and gratitude in any challenge or crisis I have faced.

An important distinction to make as you write your new story is that faith and fear cannot exist together. You can't have both at the same time. As you go through this book and your life, simply set the intention that you will choose faith over fear. If you are faced with emotional turmoil or making tough decisions ask, "What would faith say?" instead of "What does fear say?" It will allow your newfound awareness to help you make better choices. As you make decisions it is important to see how tricky fear or your Little Voice can be. You may have been guided by fear for so long you don't even know what it looks like.

For example, if you are afraid of making the wrong decision in ending a relationship, simply choose faith that you will be guided. Quit reasoning and thinking you need to do something quickly. Write down a list of what fear says and then what faith says. Expand on this by doing the same with ego versus love. When you review it eliminate your hallucinations. An example of a hallucination that is usually a top fear might be, "I will never find anyone again."

We often let fear guide us without realizing our ego is in control. As you learned, your ego has no real desire for joy so it only seeks to protect you and gain moments of short-term pleasure. Millions of women stay in relationships or don't work on them because of fear. Speaking up about the fact that your needs aren't being met or walking out on someone who is abusive seems scary at first. If you don't like conflict or aren't strong enough to face the uncertainty of it all, then fear will keep you paralyzed. If you have faith and believe that God or the Universe will guide you through this transition, then you will find the courage to move on and likely end up growing because of it.

Choosing faith over fear is a big part of your TMS. It is a daily requirement. We worry and hypothesize way too much. This heaviness that we carry steals our joy. When you face decisions or are entrenched in thinking too much, you simply need to stop and become aware that you have a choice. Again, ask yourself what fear would say. Then contrast it with what faith would say. You will always see faith is a much better decision.

Unfortunately, a lot of our fear is societal and is inappropriate fear. Fear can cause a rise in adrenaline. We can kick ourselves into fight or flight mode without really being in danger. This raises our stress hormones (cortisol) and leaves us fatigued. Fears of rejection or failure are common in many women. We have to learn to accept rejection and failure as stepping stones to growth. Without them, we stay too comfortable and become complacent.

We have a choice and can make a decision to not let fear guide us. It will keep us small and feeling helpless. For those that live in areas or are in relationships that warrant appropriate fear, i.e. life threatening situations, I pray you can create a plan that will lead you to safety. Having helped many women through this I know it is a complicated decision. God will catch you when you have faith and open doors you didn't know would open. You will feel guided and supported, even when fear is trying to paralyze you.

Surrendering and Managing Freewill

Surrendering our own decision making and trusting God or the Universe to lead us is scary to do. We all desire to be in control and we lack the trust needed to know everything will be okay. We are obsessed with replaying the past and hypothesizing about our future. But here is life's greatest secret – this is all a waste of time and it will steal all your joy. It is a trap set by your Little Voice to keep you paralyzed with fear and regret. It is like a prison that you know you don't like living in, yet you aren't quite sure how to get out.

The past can leave clues which can be helpful to expose patterns you want to break. Taking into consideration your future self so you don't make impulsive decisions is positive as well. That is not usually what we are doing. We are reliving life scene by scene, trying to make rational sense of a feeling or emotion we are having. We want something or someone to blame. When we fret about our future and are not trusting of God our worry affects our physical and emotional state.

Falling into a place where you feel your life is guided will not be easy. You have to give up the addiction to thinking and use your awareness to be grounded. Even if you aren't a religious person, knowing there is a universal force working for your good will help you let go.

I wish I could share a step by step approach to surrendering. My journey was filled with painful disappointments that finally led to an ultimate decision that I had zero idea what I was doing and needed someone to guide me. I was competent in many areas, but I sucked at relationships. I was creating my own self-suffering that was causing fatigue. The fatigue was distracting me from my purpose, so I knew something wasn't right. I had been talking myself into a relationship instead of feeling my way into it.

God will show you what is right, but you have to be open to his guidance. I fought it over and over because so many of my other needs were being met. It wasn't until my last partner and I had compatibility issues from which I couldn't recover that I was guided to end the relationship and fully surrender again.

I discovered a book by accident called *Power of I AM*, by Joel Olsteen, that changed how I viewed myself. I almost didn't buy it because I had been practicing "I am" statements for over 10 years. After I read it, I realized deep down I didn't value myself enough to believe I deserved an amazing man or to have it all. As my business coach Theresa Jabbour from Mark Kamin and Associates said, I didn't think I could have it all and be a 10 out of 10 in all areas of my life.

I was choosing men that hadn't actualized their purpose or potential. I wanted so badly to be a person who didn't care about money or achievement because I had classified them as ego and significance-driven. I ignored many red flags because I was trying to force things too much. What I found through hours of self-discovery is that my authentic self is highly driven which creates success and an abundance of prosperity for me. I hadn't managed it well internally though, because again, deep down I didn't feel worthy or confident. This was showing up not only at work but also in relationships. I was afraid I didn't deserve success and an amazing relationship. It was almost as if I thought I had to sacrifice one for the other.

I have also wondered if some of this came out of guilt that my sister was struggling in so many areas of her life. I had thought I was so confident and had high self-worth until this revelation shattered my understanding of myself. I had been creating so much self-suffering out of fear. Fear of going back to the significance-driven girl who discarded people that didn't add value. I had just built a newly improved false self through my personal growth journey. Externally, my mindset and life shifted, but internally I still didn't feel right. The truth is it took me years to fully feel like I deserved everything that I had.

Fully surrendering is a final letting go of any attachment, guilt, shame, or fear and becoming aware the present moment is the most valuable. It is letting go of regret and anxiousness about your future. You can be committed to learning from your past but only with compassion for all your mistakes. You can have goals and a plan for your future but also accept nothing is truly within your control.

Surrendering equals trust. You trust life will bring you problems and disappointments, but you are emotionally resilient. Anytime you face a problem you gain strength from a higher power. Surrendering is a decision that you will have to make day after day. It gives you the power and strength to let the monkeys hang out, knowing they will pass and not criticizing yourself for not being able to stop them.

If you want to change or write a new story because you hate yourself, you are not on the right path. This means you aren't yet in your Big Voice because if you were you would love yourself completely and have compassion for where you are currently. You would finally walk around feeling like a masterpiece that is allowed to make mistakes. You would no longer try to force anything and you would let life flow around you. You would trust your body to guide you so that you feel energized and on the right path. Change and grow because you seek more not because you hate yourself.

All the "I want, I want, I want" needs are left behind. You remain present and don't have the false idea anything external can fill you up. You quit spending time calculating or anticipating the future because you are content to live in this moment. You have a vision and discipline that keeps you rooted in your authenticity so self-sabotage doesn't get in your way.

Surrendering causes tremendous discomfort. It goes against patterns and preferences your ego and Little Voice created. They are not patient and trusting. They want you to believe that you have to do everything and that when you are present something must be wrong. In this state, using metaphors to symbolize the past and future can help see these thoughts and emotions for what they are. Visualize something separate from yourself like a helium balloon or heavy weight you are pulling; something that is connected to you but completely separate and not in control. You have so much more ability to quiet these distractions if you can see them disconnected from your Big Voice. My monkeys show up every day to try to steal my joy, but I am armed against them. I am completely shielded by sheer determination that they will have no effect on my actions.

Beyond being uncomfortable, surrender can often feel like defeat. You should expect to lose some inspiration or energy initially if you have always relied only on yourself. You may have to go through a mourning period after you realize your Little Voice has lost its power. There might be some shame or guilt over all the choices, anxiety, or stress your false-self created, but trust that your past unfolded exactly as it was supposed to. The timing is perfect. This is your divine time to write a new story.

Curiosity is necessary to understand what you really want in life and identify negative patterns in your past. It is a new lens you use to look backwards to find common thought patterns or choices with the intention to learn not who or what to blame but only how you can create more joy today.

This is common for many people. We relive a movie reel of our life and become emotionally triggered easily by wounds from the past. We want to figure out our failures or mistakes like a puzzle to solve. We want to blame others like our parents, ex-partner, or anyone in the script who had a negative effect on us. It can be easier to link our current state to a past event. If we were abandoned or rejected, we can blame our closed heart on that. If we are passive, we can blame the chaotic childhood we had. If we feel guilty or ashamed, we can blame our religious upbringing. We can always find something in our past to blame. Your new story needs to leave this need to blame behind.

I could easily say the reason I am divorced and have a monkey-mind when it comes to relationships is because I grew up with a father who objectified women and a mother who was controlling and dominant. I had the false belief I needed to be with an impressive man to be important. I could blame my sister for being in an volatile relationship which might explain why I was so guarded since I never wanted to be that stupid or vulnerable. I could blame my mother for not teaching me how to be feminine or loving to a partner. I could blame my grandma for how fiercely independent she was. I could blame the movies I watched that fantasized Prince Charming rescuing the damsel in distress. I could blame the rejection I felt if a boy didn't like me the way I liked him. I could blame my first relationship that went too fast and left me embarrassed when he cheated on me. Do you see where I am going with this?

If we look back seeking blame, there is plenty of it to choose from. Choosing to look back with curiosity rather than blame will minimize suffering. When I use this lens, I see things differently. I am curious how my dad constantly checking out women formed a false belief that my external appearance was more important than who I was inside. I see how my craving for more attention or significance may have been formed. If I wasn't being checked-out or given attention there must be something wrong with me.

I see how if I wasn't getting attention I might make up stories about out-of-town boyfriends in fear I wasn't good enough. I see how my fear of rejection created a strong ego that protected me from pain. I see how being closed-off led me to more shallow emotional relationships with people that could not hurt me. I see how my false belief that I needed a relationship might have come from believing this determined your worth. This unhealthy belief may have caused more heartache and rejection than had I allowed myself to be fully open and whole on my own. When having a relationship is more important to you than who the relationship is with, you are setting yourself up for suffering. As you write your new story and find your Big Voice just be sure to always remain curious about your past rather than being obsessed with it or thinking you should have done anything differently.

Surrendering our decision making and trusting that God or the Universe will lead us down the right path may feel like surrendering our power. It is true. He has given us instructions or commandments that are found in religious or spiritual teachings. No matter what book you pick up, the *Bible, Book of Buddha, the Torah, Tao Te ching, Koran*, etc., there are principles and similarities in all of them that stand the test of time. In spite of this guidance, He does not force us to follow any rules. God gave each of us freewill to make our own decisions – only one of which is to trust in Him and let Him guide our life.

This freewill varies from person to person

because we all were born into different families, communities, or religions. Some of us were raised with God and others without. Freewill suggests you can make choices and live any way you want. It typically guides you to pleasure seeking rather than creating joy. It also means it is up to you to create your purpose, find your passion, and use willpower to avoid bad decisions.

If you look around the world, freewill has gotten us into a severely shattered state. We are depressed, disconnected, and worn out. Society has created bars for success that are impossible for most to reach. To top it off, many people often deemed successful aren't usually humble, kind, or emotionally fulfilled.

Freewill has also devastated our union with God. We are quite picky and choosy when we need Him. Many pray for solutions to problems or miracles only when someone is sick or in trouble. We spend most of our time on a smart phone, but don't take time to talk to our Creator. We are self-obsessed, impulsive, and reactive humans.

The campaign, "Have It Your Way" by Burger King is a great illustration of how most people live on earth. As our choice to choose freewill over God has risen, so has suffering. Both self-induced suffering and suffering created by others. They are ultimately tied together. Eventually, someone suffering internally will need to release the trapped pain and take it out on others. When I see criminals commit acts of violence my thought is, *of course they did. It was just a matter of time.* You can usually find clues in their behavior or actions long before a crime is committed.

Surrendering is the most liberating choice you can make on your spiritual journey. To make the decision to give up freewill means you acknowledge you have very little control in this world and you trust God completely to guide you. You may even surrender over and over again as you identify different areas where you need to let go. As you widen life experiences or relationships you open yourself to more problems or overthinking. At first I craved peace and thought I would get it from living a simple life until I found out that was not my purpose and God guided me into more troubled waters.

Surrender feels like falling to your knees, giving up, letting go, stopping the fight, and filling with God's glory all at the same time. It is a magical state that I hope all of us feel one day. The original awareness and shift you felt when you wanted more meaning or saw you needed to change the way you were living, opened up a door to explore a new way. That was just the first baby step.

Getting to total surrender is a marathon. You will experience ups and downs as you awaken. Expect to take two steps forward and one step back. It may only seem like being awake is harder as you take inventory of all the wasted time or regret. You must to remember to use humor and self-compassion to ensure it doesn't feel hard. You may get more anxious and want your purpose to unfold faster. These are all normal parts of this journey. Your ego and Little Voice dominated you, so breaking these habits and pathways isn't easy. You may even go back multiple times before you fully decide to surrender. Life's struggles can overcome you. You might get confused about what's most important again. Your old patterns of thinking or doing are deep in your brain; only discipline will get you through.

I had never experienced the level of joy or freedom I have now before I surrendered. Lifting the pressure and stress of figuring things out off my shoulders was amazing. Learning to pray when problems happened instead of thinking too much increased the energy levels I had to face them. Trusting that God figures everything out for me took the responsibility off me. This doesn't mean you can sit on the couch and expect He will provide for you. You still need to take action. You just need to be conscious of how He guides you and then praise Him for it.

Now that you have decided to write a new story, the next few sections will help you develop strategies to make it happen. These have worked for me and the many women I have coached. They have been taken from every book or event I have ever attended to give you the best of what I have found, specifically for women. These strategies will help you prioritize what is most important to you so that you can build your vision and goals around it. They will help you stay on track to live the life you want. I review my plan every morning before my kids wake up and I start my day. It has helped me remain on track and more present whereas before I let other people's needs and priorities run my life. Keep in mind that if God has a different plan for me I am fully prepared to change course. Many of the pieces of my strategy have come from God's word or guidance.

Determining Your Priorities

We often live our lives in direct opposition to our priorities. When you analyze how you spend your time it will become clear that you likely spend less time on yourself than you do on other things. The reason we can feel fatigued and guilty all the time is because we allow life to run us rather than us running our life.

If you have a relationship, career, children, aging parents, a specific charity, or friends etc. and are also trying to maintain your self-care, you know it will require commitment. At some point we just have too much on our plate and balance is impossible. We walk around in a perpetual state of never having enough time causing us suffering. We feel bad we are exhausted when we get home from work, we feel bad we never see our friends, we feel bad we are not into our partner's advance, or we feel bad it's been weeks since we worked out. Layering guilt on our already fragile and worn out self is not the answer. This pattern of doing too much rarely changes even when the circumstance change. Your kids eventually leave home, aging parents die, you may even retire, yet the incompatibility of the life you live with the priorities you want goes on. You will tend to fill the time with something else and continue to get down on yourself.

So, how can you ensure every day is intentional? How do you live your life in line with your priorities? You must get crystal clear on what they are before you create your goals or set up your daily disciplines. You must work at your priorities daily so as things come at you, you're still committed to your priorities. It is the daily choices we make that add up to a lifetime of fulfillment. It might be the five extra minutes with your child or the small habits at work that really make a difference in your level of joy.

I have 8 top priorities in my life that are also a part of my goals. They are:

1. God
2. My emotional and physical well-being
3. My children/partner
4. Family
5. Purpose
6. Career
7. Friends
8. Finances

Recently I attended the funeral of the wife of a co-worker. Niki was a young mom who went too soon. I reflected on how short life is and wondered if she had regrets. Listening to others speak about her love for her husband and kids, I felt peace knowing she got it right. I was filled with gratitude for the changes I had made in my own life. I knew that I was doing my best being a mom, ensuring my kids always knew where they stood.

Life is busy so we easily allow our priorities to be buried. We take for granted the many tomorrows that will come. Regret and shame are around the corner if you don't start living a priority-based life now. Really take some time to create your priorities and then compare them to your goals, schedule, and budget. If you aren't in alignment, you'll need to make some changes. You are creating new disciplines and it won't be easy. For me work always took priority over my physical and emotional well-being. By the time I got home I was too exhausted and empty to care for myself or give my kids my best self. I met their basic needs but was worn out. I had to make adjustments to ensure that I gave the most time and attention to my biggest priorities.

After you finish your priorities then it is time to do your vision, goals, and daily disciplines. Even when I form new habits I never stop having them as a part of my plan. Our human tendency is to resort to old patterns even if we have the best of intentions. I make sure I am dedicating time to each priority based on their importance in my life. For example, my relationship with God has deepened since I started reading the Bible every morning. I also write to Him giving Him glory for my joy and inviting Him in to heal my suffering when I journal. When I say no one can steal my joy it is because my relationship with Him is truly first. I also set new goals for my relationship with my kids. Not new goals FOR my kids but who I can BE for them. Values and wisdom are always goals for my year so I can ensure I am giving them confidence and enduring love. You are writing a new story when your priorities come first.

Clarifying Your Vision

After you are done with your priorities, you will want to create your life vision. We all seek clarity about what we really want in our life. Is this the right job or career? Am I in the right relationship? Am I being a good mom, daughter, or friend? Is there more for me? We all crave being content with knowing we lived fully, yet we often stay paralyzed in a situation that lacks joy. If you are making excuses for your life right now, you are not on the right track. Your ego or Little Voice will make it impossible to thrive without suffering. Or it will tell you tomorrow will improve as the kids get older or your partner will get better. Any idea that the future is what holds joy is not coming from your Big Voice or highest self. You need to make the decision that you have the ability to create the life you want now in spite of your circumstances. No more "if onlys" are going to stand in your way. It is time to get clear about what you want and build a plan to achieve it.

The first step in getting clear and building a plan is to develop a personal vision statement. A vision statement is defined as: *an aspirational description of what an organization would like to achieve or accomplish in the mid-term or long-term future. It is intended to serve as a clear guide for choosing current and future courses of action.* (www.businessdictionary.com). In this case the organization is you. You must have clarity around your life and your business if you want to develop sustained joy. Your vision statement should help you be more intentional about how you live your life and how you spend your time. It will help you make decisions and set boundaries. I would suggest reviewing it anytime you are not clear about whether you have capacity to do something or not. Before deciding on your personal vision, ask yourself the following questions:

- Who do you want to be?
- Where do you want to be in five or ten years?
- How do you want to feel?

The keys to creating a compelling vision statement are to dream big and use concise language. It is a living, breathing testament to how you will go about your day so it should be written in present tense. You can create a short one or make it detailed. I like to focus on the impact I make in other's lives and how I feel doing it. My latest vision statement is: with an open heart I will fearlessly share love and wisdom with the world creating more joy and less suffering. Before I had written my new story my vision was pages long. Now I have one simple statement and then individual ones for each area of my life that includes business, finances, relationships, health, parenting, etc.

There is no right or wrong way to write a vision statement. It just has to be in alignment with the overall life you want to lead. Joy has special importance for me both personally and professionally. If I can't do something with joy, I won't do it. The major thing is that it resonates with you once it's written. If you don't get excited every time you read it, then it isn't truly your vision. It is the first thing I read every morning after I am done with my devotional time.

When we are in survival mode it seems unrealistic to have a vision. It is almost as if we have given up and don't have the freedom to create the life we want. We must rise above this and get clear on what we want. For some of you, this may be easy. It is clear you want a new career or job that has more meaning. It is clear you want your kids to be more respectful. It is clear you want to become more resilient so you don't wallow in self-pity when problems hit.

For some of you this may be a bit of a mystery

at first. You know your life lacks joy, but you aren't 100 percent clear on why. You just need to start somewhere and not get trapped in the false idea something will shift on its own. If you look at this as an adventure rather than a burden you won't end up overwhelmed. Make a list of things that bring you joy and meaning and then a list of preferences not currently being met. If any of your preferences involve you growing, then add them to your annual growth plan that I will go over later. If any involve external forces like your boss respecting you more, your husband cherishing you more, or your kids behaving, build another list about how you can be more bold and clear about your needs. For example, schedule a meeting with your boss and share you want to feel more respected. Ask his advice on what you can do above and beyond what you are now to take on more. Do you need more education, training, etc. for this to happen or can you work towards a promotion? You may need others to help you clarify your vision. If your boss is supportive, then you will be able to grow and continue to find more meaning and joy in your work. If your boss is not supportive, then you are left with a choice. Either move on to a job with more joy and meaning or do it at your current job without his support.

Relationships are a bit trickier as you may find yourself in one before you are totally clear on your vision. My vision has standards including how I want to feel. I want someone growth-minded and purpose-driven that I can respect and support. I love watching a man read or improve himself. I also love when he is connected to his higher purpose and making a difference in this world. If you are single, this exercise makes it easier to not waste time when you are dating. If you are married or in a relationship, this will be more challenging if you have standards or feelings not being met. It is possible as you work on yourself, they may also grow with you.

So what do you do when your vision and reality are miles apart? You optimistically create a growth and learning plan that will shorten the gap. For anyone that says people don't change, I call utter bullshit! People change every day! One good book, the loss of a loved one, a brush with death, etc. can all shake people up. I can assure with your newly found Big Voice you can influence the state of any relationship you are in.

It is up to you if you want to let your partner know or not. There may be non-negotiables that you should give them an opportunity to address before you end it. If there are things you are working on, sharing them can help you receive feedback. Sharing your newly adopted mindset or I Am list will help someone else hold you accountable. In addition, you may have a list of things that you want to respect or admire in a partner.

Many men feel they can't do anything right for you or they are not your highest priority. In order to achieve your relationship vision, you may need to look in the mirror and start owning your part. It is easy to start feeling sorry for yourself and make things worse. This is your ego choosing blame; not your highest-self knowing how powerful and influential you are.

If there is any emotional or physical abuse, no matter how hard you have tried, you must end it. As women, these relationship lines can become blurred. Whether you feel no one else will love you or you can't manage financially, the truth is you will never "not suffer" if you stay. These relationships often create the highest highs and the lowest lows. It will split your heart in two remaining in this yo-yo. I recommend you seek help immediately and start planning for a safe departure.

If there is not any abuse and you want to make things work, you are the only one guaranteed to change at this point. You cannot rely on your partner to change unless you have created a non-negotiable standard or boundary. Here is how I would recommend creating this vision.

Begin with your purpose or mission for the relationship. For example: I want to love and share my joy with a like-minded partner where I can be respectful and nurturing. I want to live an extraordinary life with them and laugh and play hard. I want to be confident and authentic. Then add in values that are important that you share or become one in the relationship. These could be: love, passion, courage, or contribution. Finally, add on your standards or boundaries: growth-minded, has purpose and joy, and free of addictions, or whatever they might be.

Identify Your Goals

The second step in gaining clarity to become the person you are destined to be is to identify the goals that will help you attain your vision. I like to believe that everyone's ultimate vision is to live an amazing life. I define amazing as doing what you love and loving how you do it. Goal setting can propel your vision forward. When you define what an amazing life looks like you are maximizing your resources: knowledge, skills, time, and passion so you can make the most of your life and feel more fulfilled about what you're doing. When you write out your goals, you are creating an external representation of your internal desires and reinforcing their value. Setting tangible goals allows you to break those big dreams into bite-size, achievable steps.

Most important, goals hold you accountable. They get you out of the "if only" rut that steals so much of your joy and happiness: if only I made more money, if only I lost this weight, if only my business were thriving, then I'd be happy. Tangible goals help you to see and celebrate your successes.

Part of goal planning is becoming that person who is joyful and happy today even though you haven't yet achieved all you may want. If you remember when we looked at how your brain works, setting goals will also release dopamine which will help you feel physically and emotionally better. Goals should encompass your overall life not just your career. You have to find a balance because we all have multiple priorities in our life. If all you do is set goals for your career then you may be unconsciously sabotaging yourself if those goals are in conflict with your vision for your family, your relationships, or your personal development. Over many years of living this way I no longer write out as many goals as I did when I started. In addition they are now more focused on habits I want to form long-term or who I want to be rather than what I want to accomplish. I do recommend if you have not done goals before to start with only a couple in each category to prevent yourself from becoming overwhelmed.

Goal Setting Process

The method I use to do goal planning is a simple four step process:

1. Make a commitment. Too many people write down goals and then never follow through on them. Just like those New Year's resolutions that last only a week or two. If you are serious about creating an extraordinary life you must be committed to attaining the goals you set for yourself. You have to say, "for the next 3 months, 6 months, 12 months, I'm going to entrench myself in living this goal." You are committed to sitting down with them every single day, reviewing them and checking-in with yourself to see if you're getting closer to or farther away from what you want to achieve.

2. Identify what you really want. Get really clear about this. What do you want to achieve? What types of people do you want to work with? How do you want to feel? What do you want to change in your mindset or in your sabotaging behaviors? What outputs or outcomes are desired?

3. Recognizing why you want it. If you are going to stay committed you have to understand why you want the things you want. Most people will say something like, "Well, I want to make $20,000 a month." That's great but I push them farther to get to the underlying reason why $20,000 is important. What does it mean to make that money? Well it could mean they can save money for retirement so they can live the life they want, or it might mean being able to put their children through college, or maybe it allows them to take the vacations they've always wanted, or pay off debt that's been holding them back. The deeper you can get into the "why" of the wanting, the more leverage you'll have and the more committed you will be to following through on the activities necessary to accomplish your goals. Be careful that fear is not your leverage.

4. Create a plan in order to achieve them. Plain and simple, if you don't plan your life, it will be controlled by other people's demands and priorities. Unless we have tangible results from the activities we engage in – whether it's spending time on social media, cultivating new relationships, or working on our career – our brain will not remember why it's supposed to keep doing these things. That's why it's so important to be disciplined about setting our goals and executing a plan to obtain them.

Goals need to be the right goals. They need to be S.M.A.R.T. This acronym was first written down in November, 1981 by consultant George T. Doran in a paper he published entitled, "There's a S.M.A.R.T. Way to Write Management Goals and Objectives." It stands for: Specific, Measurable, Action-Oriented, Realistic, and Time Sensitive. Each goal should be written with these five things in mind.

Specific: getting exceptionally clear about what you are going to accomplish. I learned this lesson in a funny way. I wrote down one year that I wanted to be on Oprah's show but didn't specify what I meant. In my mind, I wanted to be a guest being interviewed about a book that wasn't yet written. At the end of that year when we were both guests of Tony Robbins at his Unleash the Power Within event my goal came true. Oprah captured me about eight times on film since I was sitting by her and she was filming a special about the event. I was on the Oprah show multiple times but it wasn't really what I had in mind. I did get to walk on fire with her which was life changing but the goal in my head wasn't specific enough. Ironically this is still a goal but now is clear that I want to be on Super Soul Sunday to talk about mainstream mindfulness and this book.

Measurable: Remember the adage – inspect what you expect. You are trying to build feelings of success. You need to set goals that allow you to see the progress you are making.

I like to put my mindset goals on a spectrum of one to ten where ten is the desired result. Take the goal of feeling abundance for example. Imagine a spectrum where scarcity is a one and total feeling of abundance is a ten. Every day you can assess where you are on that scale. Maybe you're a four today. You are still worried about being able to pay your bills. If some deals don't close you get anxiety when you go to the grocery store and swipe your debit card, even though you know that there's money in your account. Over time as you build up a reserve account, when you get to where you're feeling a seven or an eight, you will know that your mindset has shifted and you have grown through scarcity. You've earmarked money for groceries and vacations and you're supposed to be spending money on these things.

Another example might be a goal of resilience where one is being not resilient at all, losing my shit every single day, and ten being everything just rolls off me like a duck. It's all about asking daily, where am I today? Where am I trying to move myself on that needle?

Action-Oriented: Nothing gets done if you don't take action. Contrary to information found in *The Secret* you can't wish it and it will come. That's not to say that a golden egg will never land in your lap, but you'll have far more eggs if you actively go out and collect them. You know your life is guided when you are clear as to what you want and you take the action necessary to move forward.

Realistic: It helps to make sure your goals are realistic before you start taking action on them. When your goals are unrealistic your brain knows it. You'll only end up in a place of excuse making and self-sabotage. Do you have enough time? Do you have the skills? Do you have the right connections to make it happen? We all might have a goal of being on *The Voice* but if God didn't give us a beautiful voice, it is not going to happen.

Time Sensitive: If something is going to get accomplished it must have a deadline. I do my goals quarterly not annually and have set dates for completion. Most of us are procrastinators and if we have deadlines we will push harder to accomplish our goal. Take my final book edits . . . I am typing this sentence 24 hours before my final copy is due.

In order to maintain balance and not allow your goals to conflict with each other, it helps to put them in four categories: Business, Financial, Health, and Family/Relationships. You can expand on these categories as much as you want but I have found keeping things simple helps. To make it easy you can download a Goal Setting and Action Steps worksheet at BigVoicesRise.com

You should create a few short-term (3 months) and a few long-term (12 months) goals for each category. Next identify the top action steps you're going to take to accomplish each goal. Then finally, you'll want to identify what you want to avoid the most and the top way that you typically sabotage yourself in meeting this goal. We will cover this more in depth later as we create a Sabotage Management Strategy and review Away from Values but here is an overview.

These are what I call "away values." They are things you are patterned to do that no longer serve you. I first came across this term when studying NLP – Neuro Linguistic Programming. NLP is taught by the Empowerment Partnership and is a method of teaching your conscious mind the language of your unconscious mind. Examples of away values would be passivity, perfectionism, judgement – any of your sabotage methods.

For business one of my top away values is being passive. I want to really be able to speak up and not worry about how others see me. I don't want to swallow whatever I'm thinking in fear others won't agree. It also wants everyone to love me. It can make me passive at times. It makes me believe that everything has to be perfect before I move forward with a goal or plan.

I like to keep all of my goals in one place so I can easily review them often. I use a journal to do this with each category having its own page. Every morning after I wake up and have had my devotional time, I take out my journal and review all my I AM statements, my vision, my values (both those I want to keep and those I want to eliminate), and my goals. After that I journal. I redo my goals every three months since that's about what my journal will hold. Some people prefer a one page goal sheet or others a vision board. It doesn't really matter what form you use to keep your goals as long as they are easy to access and you commit to a daily morning review.

I'm going to reiterate the importance of reviewing your goals every day. If you do so, you'll drive the concepts of what you want to accomplish deeper into your subconscious and conscious mind so they become more patterned. Contrary to popular opinion, it's not about repro-gramming your brain; it's about programming it for the first time. Your brain wants to take the path of least resistance so it will react based on past experience. It is so lazy! But if you set your goals deeper with really great intentions and leverage behind them, then your brain will react with that intent.

For example, if your goal is to be a kinder person, you can decide in the morning the ways you might be able to do that. You need to ask yourself, how can I practice being more kind? How can I dedicate five minutes every morning just to kindness? Perhaps you could send a gratitude email to every person who made a difference to you the previous day.

Once you've written down your goals and you're comfortable that they are realistic and not in conflict with each other, I DON'T want you to commit to them right away. I always recommend that you sit with these goals and let them marinate a bit. You could cook a steak as soon as you bring it home, but if you marinate it for a while it's probably going to taste better. Do them initially and put them away. Then come back a week later and reevaluate them. Although you haven't looked at them or acted on them, subconsciously your mind will have been thinking about them. Ask yourself these questions:

Are these really my goals or what is expected of me from my family, my boss, society, or anyone else?
If you can't answer yes, then the goal is not a good

goal and you are setting yourself up for failure. If the goal isn't coming from your higher purpose, your desire, or what you envision for your life, then you will be lacking the leverage and the dedication required to take the actions that will get you there.

Are these goals aligned with my core values?

For example, if you know you have a core value of balance but you're working 60 hours a week to reach an unrealistic business or financial goal, then those are going to be in conflict with each other. You're not going to have the time to nurture relationships if you're a workaholic. I strongly recommend that you get clear on your value system even before you put together your vision. Identify the top five values for your career and for your life.

How much time do you have to allocate to your goals?

Do you actually have enough time in your day, week, or month to accomplish all your goals? You want to make sure that the goals you set are achievable given that there are only 1,440 minutes in every day and part of that time you need to sleep.

Does this goal provide the feeling or outcome you want to achieve and will it sustain you long-term?

I always say if your goals aren't life or death, don't

write them down. Don't approach goal planning with just a lighthearted, "Oh it would be fabulous if I were able to do that." Not taking action on the goals you set is more devastating to your psyche than if you didn't set them at all.

Creating a Growth Plan

Having tangible goals will go a long way to helping you attain your vision. But sometimes the goals you have require skill sets or knowledge that you may not currently possess. That's why it is very important to develop a growth plan along with your goals and vision.

You'll want to look closely at your goals and come up with a list of areas you really want to focus on for the year. Remember, not all of your goals, and certainly not your vision, need to be accomplished in one calendar year. Your growth plan however, should be.

As you develop the list, you can start researching authors, speakers, or events that are designed to help individuals grow in this area. Then you'll need to create the time each week to dedicate to these activities. It may be attending an event, reading, or spending time with others that are experts in the area – ultimately you get to choose how you will do it.

Growing is a journey and if you are anything like me your first instinct will be to throw yourself into solving the areas you have for improvement like a problem or task. This is not how it works. We are often powerless to truly change ourselves and instead must invite God in to help us. You must trust that people or situations will come to you that will help you grow in whatever areas you have identified. You also do not want to become overwhelmed believing you can grow through everything at once.

When I started my awakening in 2003, I sat down and made a list of my goals. I knew like the foundation of a home that my physical health had to come first. I was not going to be able to tackle the other areas until I had more energy and felt better. As soon as I made that decision, people came into my life that helped me learn more about why I was unhealthy. Over the next several years, I threw away my scale and stopped eating meat and sugar. My health has not been a challenge since. Eating healthy and exercising are habits now. This means I don't even think about what I need to do daily. In other areas though, I still must be intentional. I am challenged daily with caring too much about what other people think but can see it clearly now. When I feel this happening, I just smile and laugh at how silly it is. I still dedicate time for learning more about how to overcome my away from values and love reading stories about other women that have overcome their self-suffering. This ensures I remain hopeful that overtime these things will show up less and less in my life.

With my personality, if I didn't do an annual plan for growth, I would try to focus on too many things and never get anywhere. If you are like me, OR you have been procrastinating on dealing with things about yourself that no longer serve you, an annual growth plan is right for you too. You can find an Annual Growth Plan on the Big Voices website – BigVoicesRise.com

Commitment to Discipline

I've talked several times about having discipline. Discipline and positive habits are what all awakened and successful women have in common. We know what we need to do every day even if we don't feel like it. Discipline is only hard if you think about it too much. This is the secret that I have found amongst most successful women . . . nobody really feels like eating kale to stay healthy but we do because it is good for us. I mean seriously, if you are one of those women who actually like kale I think you are crazy! It's not typically yummy or easy to choose over French fries. If I waited until I felt like eating kale I never would, so instead I use discipline to make it a normal part of my diet.

Motivation is doing what needs to be done when we *want* to do it. You need to let go of the notion that we will always be motivated. It's unlikely that you're going to wake up every morning wanting to do the mundane tasks that need to be done. But you keep hoping that you will. And then you beat yourself up when you don't do what you know you should. You get caught in this perpetual loop that always ends in you being disappointed in yourself. You have to be able to love yourself before you can love and be of service to others. You must walk away from the notion of motivation. I use a non-negotiable activity planner to ensure I complete everything that needs to be done regardless of how I am feeling.

What you should do instead is rely on discipline. Don't get me wrong. I love motivation. I wish we could all be more motivated. Discipline is what gets us through by doing what needs to be done when it needs to be done even when we *don't want* to do it. Relying on discipline rather than motivation will in fact take you where you want to be.

For example, no matter what I get up at 6 a.m. I

spend an hour on mindset, on prayer, on other things that I know are going to put me in a state of joy. I need to be in this state because I'm attacked daily – things come at me. I'm running a sales team and supporting other people. My kids are moody and not always grateful. I've got to be in a state where nobody steals my joy. Are you in that state? If not, then you need to get yourself there.

MINDSET AND CORE BELIEFS

"We live in an epoch in which the solid ground of our preconceived ideas shakes daily under our certain feet."
Barbara Ward

After your priorities are set, goals made, and plan created, if you don't have the right mindset and core beliefs the likelihood of sticking to your new story is unlikely. So many people believe mindset is only important in business, but it is important in every area of our life. Mindset can be defined as your perceptions or the core beliefs an individual has about life and all its circumstances.

Core beliefs begin in childhood and develop over time. They are the essence of how we see ourselves, other people, the world, and the future. Our core beliefs often stem from the values of our families and the communities we grew up in. They can be deeply rooted, rigid, and inflexible. This inflexibility leads us to focus on those things that support our beliefs and dismiss or ignore evidence that contradicts them.

Many of us don't know what our mindset is because we've lived with our core beliefs so long that we are no longer consciously aware of them. When you find yourself ready to write a new story, you will need to see what your current mindset is and either create a new one or make modifications to your existing one. If there is one thing that I see that separates those that experience success and those that don't, it is having the right outlook. You can shift your beliefs even if many of them have been limiting your potential forever. You can challenge your thinking and replace it with thoughts and beliefs that serve your greater good.

One of the easiest ways to begin to uncover those core beliefs that no longer serve you is to pay attention to the words or dialogues that come out of your mouth or the unspoken thoughts you are having. Are you always complaining? Are you quick to place blame? Are you always judging other people? The more you pay attention to the negative things you say or think, the more you can ask, "Why am I feeling this way?" Emotions and the feelings behind those emotions are the keys to discovering what you truly believe. When you understand what you believe and why you believe it, you have the ability to change that belief for the better.

Big Voice Mindset

The mindset of a spiritually successful woman with a Big Voice includes the following attributes: growth-minded, value-driven, goal-oriented, optimistic, awake, manages thoughts/emotions, loves herself, is grateful and detached. She has a "in spite of" view. In spite of any suffering, problems, or negativity she will choose joy, hope, and faith. A Big Voice mindset knows that love is the most important thing we have on earth. Some of the core beliefs are: I cannot please everyone, I don't take things personally, I know other people do the best they can, I must forgive myself and everyone else, and it is okay to say No and set boundaries. If you haven't already, it is time to adopt this mindset for yourself. You might not ever feel 100% that way but it is a good target to shoot for.

Every day you have to step into this mindset and set daily reminders if needed to get back on track. If you encounter stress or triggers, simply breathe for a moment and don't react. The goal is to respond after you have taken a moment or some time to think through the best way to handle whatever situation has arisen.

We often want instant results, but this is not possible. It will take time to fully become the unique person we were intended to become before our environment and society programmed us in error. God made us all a masterpiece with a specific purpose. Being patient through the process of realizing this is critical. As I was listening to inspirational author Louise Hay's interview on Hay House, I became hopeful that there would be a point in time when all of my awareness and wisdom would finally be in alignment with my thoughts.

Louise has since passed away but she oozed a sense of self-confidence that is rare. Her life had been devoted to people suffering both physically and emotionally. She was one of the early thought leaders in the consciousness movement before anyone even knew what it was. There are parts of her work I disagree with but I do agree we are more beautiful and powerful than we give ourselves credit for. I work on my mindset every day and focus on gratitude. Even though I do this, I can still have thoughts and emotions that don't serve me. Louise gave me hope that one day I will let go of trying to control it.

As you review your mindset and identify areas you can grow in just add them to your Annual Growth Plan remembering you cannot focus on everything at once. The beliefs or attributes will give you a new lens to compare your current thinking to as situations arise. If you focus on one area at a time you are less likely to become overwhelmed. It is important to accept and love yourself in spite of any work you want to do. Sometimes you might just have to make a tough decision that the work needed is too much to deal with right now.

As I was building my mindset, a huge area I had to master was detachment. I was constantly disappointed professionally when a deal fell apart especially if I made any mistakes or someone decided not to work with me. I took it personally and it affected my emotional and physical health. I was super sensitive to other people's opinions and I had a deep belief I needed to be perfect. I also had expectations for people in my personal life, and for events and vacations. My frontal lobe simulated both worst and best case scenarios very well. Because of this, I would be left without a lot of joy and a lot of disappointment.

Around 2006 I found Deepak Chopra's, *The Seven Spiritual Laws of Success*. Although I love all the laws, the Law of Detachment resonated with me most. I could see how my over-stimulated frontal lobe left me attached rather than detached to most outcomes. Suggestions like the universe will dance when I accept the uncertainty life brings was just the reminder I needed that I was trying to control my life too much. It was no wonder I was never content.

At the time, I didn't have growth goals or a well-defined mindset, but I knew if I could become more detached I would have more peace. I made a decision to focus that entire year on being more detached. I read his law every day and set my intentions for how I could practice it. At the time, my family was struggling with my mom's dementia. She was still trying to maintain some independence, but was getting disoriented and lost more often. It caused a lot of stress for me with my dad and I was getting frustrated with him regularly. I was busy with a two-year-old, a newborn, my business, and a new house. Becoming detached allowed me to handle all of these competing priorities easier without becoming stressed out. I knew rationally that my dad was doing the best he could, but my Little Voice kept triggering an expectation he could do better. My mom was always put together before she got sick but in his care she wore no make-up and her hair was never done. Seriously I don't think I ever saw her without lipstick on before that . . . I actually think she slept with it on. My heart hurt every time I saw her because she looked so different. It was work letting go and accepting the situation for what it was. I just moved on and started doing her hair and make-up when I saw her and didn't take it out on my dad. I also had to laugh at how ridiculous my preference was that she looked healthy even though I knew she was not.

Becoming detached also helped my business tremendously. I was no longer being thrown off by rejection or complaints. I simply accepted my team did the best we could and would learn from every challenge or mistake. It made my clients and referral partners see that the mindset of our entire team was always committed to growth and innovation and in turn created more opportunity for us. We never blamed anyone else and always owned whatever our client's perception was.

I knew I had many other areas I could grow in as well, but I faced them in order of importance based on the season I was in and the capacity I had. The year after detachment I tackled becoming more present, awake, and mindful. This is always work for me which is proof that even if you learn everything there is to know about a particular belief you might continue to struggle with it.

A spiritually successful woman knows she can only celebrate awareness and have no expectation that suffering will end. She knows that she has to work on who she is to prepare for anything life brings her. She knows life will give her the same opportunities over and over again until she fully embraces life's lessons. She knows her mindset will determine the quality of her life. She knows her physical and emotional health must be prioritized over everyone else so she can be strong and intentional for those she loves and supports. She knows to ask for help and be vulnerable. She knows being honest and authentic will release her from stress. She knows when she looks in the mirror she must honor and accept her God-given beauty. She knows she cannot please everyone and will only lose herself if she tries. She accepts prioritizing God, love, and family above all else is what is required to live her best life. She knows judging others is not her job and she will accept everyone for who they are. She knows thinking is nothing she can control, but she will practice managing her thoughts better.

You cannot control this journey, only set new intentions for your life and how you respond to things. You can only have the vision of who you want to become and then make an effort to get there. You have to remember that challenges will still happen but you can become stronger through them. You have to trust God that He will guide you and new wisdom will fall in your lap. You also need to bring love and laughter along with you to ensure it is not harder than it needs to be.

I had always known I cared too much about other people's opinions, but it wasn't until I stumbled upon Brené Brown's work in 2010 that I fully understood my perfectionism. She explains it as a form of armor, and until then I didn't know how hard I was working to protect and prove myself. She also says it is not striving to be your best or is about healthy achievement and growth. Rather it is the belief that if we live perfect we can avoid or minimize blame, judgement and shame. I guess I wasn't ready to deal with my shame or how it was connected to my perfectionism until then. When I tried changing before my Little Voice still had power. It wanted to be the "perfect" spiritually successful woman that possessed the most wisdom and whose life was proof of it. Once I found her work, I realized that I needed to go deeper and find the right "why" for going on this journey.

You have to trust with a Big Voice mindset life will start happening for you. People, information, or events will appear with everything you need to learn and see. All you have to do is be present and open. You can't force it or you will spin yourself out trying too hard to change. In addition to the core beliefs and attributes, there are some top driving values that are also important to your new mindset that we will explore next.

Endurance, Faith, and Resilience

These are all values of a successful mindset that you need to strengthen. The journey of choosing joy over suffering requires that you are intentional about increasing your values as well. You will undoubtedly face loss, tragedy, and seasons of hopelessness. Your life may be simple now, but you never know what will happen. You will need these values on your journey.

Your strength will increase as you make these values a priority in your life. Whether you need more of them right now or don't, making a decision to start focusing on them is critical. Just like training for a marathon you will need to create a plan. *Wikipedia* defines endurance as the ability of an organism to exert itself and remain active for a long period of time, as well as its ability to recover from and have immunity to trauma, wounds, or fatigue. So in short, you must train to handle more. In this context, you are increasing your emotional endurance and ability to remain in joy regardless of any external disturbances.

We can get a false sense of confidence when

everything is going right. We have energy and peace because our environment is within our control. That is honestly how most of us would prefer to live. The reality is that it doesn't last. Rather than stay in a utopic situation, to train we must push outside our comfort zone. This might be having tough conversations, reaching for our dreams, or volunteering in a place where people are suffering. We cannot grow to our potential if we are unwilling to face some uncertainty and discomfort.

I had no idea when my mom was diagnosed with dementia in 2001 that her illness would mean ten years with her before she went to heaven. Based on my early research, I thought we had five years. The first few years were tough because my dad didn't want to admit she was sick. I was not emotionally prepared for how hard it would be. We had to sell their business and real estate holdings because she had always handled all the bookkeeping. The endurance I needed to handle each day was tremendous. I was training myself to be patient, kind, and compassionate in spite of the situations and sadness her illness brought me. It took great endurance to witness her suffering and process grief at the same time.

We won't know when we will need resilience until something tragic happens. My new mindset that prioritizes love over everything else gives me the power I need to wake up every day committed to growing and feeling grateful in spite of what is going on. As I experienced new feelings, I was able to research and study my own psychology to better understand what I might be going through. I had to fight off feelings like resentment and anger towards God, my dad, and my sister. I had to learn to be present with my mom and patient. Watching a competent and strong woman's mind weaken and get worse day by day is one of the greatest teachers you can imagine. Her ego diminished with each day and what she had thought defined her faded. Her job and wealth were no longer important. Her body and her appearance didn't matter anymore. Her constant busyness had ended. It all went away as her disease took over her brain. The best part of it all was that she forgot she wanted to be thin and started eating dessert before everything else. I wouldn't wish this illness on anyone but it was a great teacher for me.

It is challenging to maintain faith in a world that tells you what you should have or need putting it always just out of your reach. Society has built so many worries, preferences, and beliefs in us that often our lives seem hopeless to enjoy fully. We grew up with ideas and preferences for our lifestyle, body, relationships, children, bank accounts, etc. Regardless of our life, we can never lose faith that we have the power to change things for the better.

Endurance, faith and resilience will be needed one day especially as we deal with our children growing up, our parents aging, or our own health issues. Strengthening them now will help make whatever you face in the future that much easier to handle. I had no idea that this would be what got me through the worst of things with my sister and allowed me to be supportive to her children.

"God will strengthen you with His own great power. And you will not give up when troubles come, but you will be patient." Colossians 1:11

Power of I AM Statements

One thing that works for me in maintaining a positive and successful mindset is to focus on a series of "I AM" statements each morning. These are statements that describe who I need to be in order to stay in my Big Voice and cultivate the energy I need. For example: I am patient, I am clear, I am smart, I am courageous, I am grateful, I am helpful, I am prospering, I am disciplined, I am . . . .

I encourage you to make your own list of I AM statements centered on the areas you feel you need to focus. Spend a few moments with them every day and begin to internalize them. In this way you will be building a mindset that has you focused on becoming the things you wish to become.

To get you started I've put together a daily mantra of I AM statements.

I am ready for this day. I am equipped and empowered. I am not going to let anyone steal my joy. I am focused on things that are in alignment with my goals or mission. I am focused and clear on what I need to execute today. I will not allow triggers to disrupt my plan.

You can then go through and add any beliefs or values that you want to strengthen such as I am Peaceful, I am Confident, I am Healthy, etc. My list that I review every day contains about twenty I Am Statements. This will help drive these core beliefs deeper into your mindset and set you up for a more intentional day.

Trigger Management Plan
A trigger is an event or thing that causes an emotional disturbance within you – fear, envy, scarcity, anger, frustration, etc. Triggers may also cause joyful reactions but most people don't need help dealing with the good stuff.

Triggers that cause negative emotions tend to make us react, usually in a negative way. What we need to learn is to identify our triggers upfront and then have a plan or an approach in place so that we choose to respond rather than react.

Reacting is allowing the emotion to guide your actions immediately without thinking about the consequences. You might yell, shut down, or send a nasty email. Responding, on the other hand, is waiting until you have assessed the situation and calmed down before you take any action. If you see this as something that derails you the following four step process may help.

Step 1 – Become aware you are triggered.
Acknowledge that you are emotionally disturbed and have a choice to either react or respond. By emotionally disturbed I mean things like: you are angry, you are frustrated, you are sad, you are depressed, you are hopeless, you feel like quitting, or whatever it is that is affecting you in the moment. What you don't want is to have that emotion or thought become a long-term feeling.

It's important to get a handle on the difference between emotions and feelings. While the words are often used interchangeably they are actually two very different things. Emotions are lower level responses to situations that cause a biochemical reaction in your body altering your physical state. Emotions are similar for all of us and include things like anger, sadness, frustration, etc. Feelings on the other hand are long-term reactions to emotions and are characteristic of our general state. Feelings are subjective. They are based on your beliefs, preferences, and personal experiences.

Becoming aware you are not your thoughts, you are not your emotions, will help you remain detached from what your body has been patterned to do based on your past experiences. Just having some space between your emotional reaction and how you handle it will allow you to be more in control. If you don't recognize these feelings they can store up and affect your ability long-term. The goal here is not to stop your emotions but direct them in a more positive way.

Step 2 – Identify Which Preference is Not Being Met. Triggers only occur when your preferences aren't being met. Most preferences are created by our ego and really aren't as important as they seem. Understanding your preferences and how they can derail you will help you grow. You can learn to be more tolerant of other's faults. You can learn to be more patient. Not all of your preferences serve you. Identifying the ones that don't and eliminating them is to your benefit.

It is an ongoing journey to manage your preferences and triggers. The fewer preferences you have based on other people's actions or behaviors, the more joy you'll have in life and your career. That's not to say you can't have standards and boundaries. They simply need to be clear and agreed to by the people with whom you interact. Then everyone knows what to expect.

In order to prevent some of this, the first thing to do is identify the preferences that trigger you regularly. Here are a few examples of preferences:

- I prefer that there be no traffic when I have to go to a meeting or be somewhere on time
- I prefer that no one makes mistakes
- I prefer that my house is clean and dinner is ready when I get home
- I prefer that my kids do their homework without being nagged and without needing my help after a long day

There is another P word that along with preferences may bring us joy or cause us suffering – Priorities. We experience deep inner conflict when we don't align our priorities with how we are living. We also suffer tremendously as our preferences steal our joy repeatedly and allow us to project blame onto others or external situations. Anytime I am struggling I ask myself these two questions: Am I spending time and energy on my priorities? Are my preferences creating irritability and complaining? Usually I find that my priorities are not straight and my preferences have caused me to be frustrated and angry at others.

Unless you love complaining or being irritated at the same things repeatedly, you should commit to growing through your most common triggers. It is almost impossible to live an extraordinary life if you get fired up all the time, especially over the same things. Getting clear that you have own your own part in your suffering helps you get out of the darkness faster.

If you're struggling to identify your preferences, it might help for you to keep a journal. Then the minute you are triggered write down what is happening and what you are feeling. Doing this provides "space" between the trigger and the action you are going to take. The difference between reacting and responding is space and awareness.

Finding your preference is uncovering what the opposite of the situation is that triggered you. Writing down what triggers me gives me space, both professionally and personally – space to see I'm emotionally triggered, space to say I could make this situation worse if I react, space to see what the best plan of action might be, and space to respond in a calm, positive manner. Dawson

Trotman, founder of The Navigators, said it like this, *"Thoughts disentangle themselves when they pass through your fingertips."* It may sound crazy but writing it down when you are pissed will help.

Step 3 – Recognize Your Hallucination. If you figure out what your hallucination is when your trigger isn't met, you will understand why it is bothering you so much. Your hallucination is the worst-case scenario that you are worried about. The goal is to have a plan that enables you to respond, not react and to admit you are hallucinating. Knowing what it is helps make it more predictable.

We all hallucinate about how bad things are. Mistakes are not the end of the world. Your brain is designed to keep you alive, not effectively handle non-life threatening situations. You need to recognize it is faulty when you are triggered. You should take a step back and remind yourself that you are not that important.

What I encourage you to do when a trigger causes you to hallucinate about all the bad things that are going to happen is to state the trigger out loud. Say, "My trigger is X because my preference of Y isn't being met, so I'm hallucinating that Z is going to happen." Just the act of saying it out loud is often enough to see the ridiculousness of what your trigger is causing you to feel. For example:

my trigger is that my son isn't doing his home-work. My preference is he completes it right after dinner before he watches TV. My hallucination is that he's never going to get into college; he's going to work at a fast food restaurant the rest of his life and live at home. When I say this out loud, before I say anything to my son, I can see how ridiculous I'm being. Again, I get the space I need to decide on a productive, positive response rather than reacting on my hallucination which wouldn't benefit either of us.

Step 4 – Avoid or Grow. The last step, and certainly the most important, is to decide to grow through the trigger or strive to avoid it. Let's take for example a preference for not getting stuck in traffic. When it happens you could choose to grow through it. You could use the time to raise your energy and do a mini-meditation, you could be more grateful, be more present, listen to a podcast, or do something else that allows you to grow and become more patient.

Or you could avoid it. You could say I'm just not going to drive at this time of day, or I'm just not going to take this route because you don't think there's any way you can grow through it. That's okay. My hope would be that you would always try to grow through it first. But we all need to give ourselves permission to draw the line when we simply can't.

It's so important to me to educate people on how to manage triggers because triggers are what derail people every day. Negative energy is what occurs when you don't manage your triggers. No one likes to work with or be around someone who has negative energy. It causes a domino effect. Maybe you get a couple of triggers strung together. Now you've had a bad day. Then you bring it home and you're not present with your family because you're still dwelling on those triggers and negative feelings. You don't exercise and you don't take care of yourself. You might then turn to food or alcohol so that you are distracted. Then later you beat yourself up for doing it. Without the ability to manage your triggers you end up creating a whirlwind of chaos.

Self-Sabotage

We all have our own preferred methods of sabotage. If you look back on your relationships or seasons when you suffered you will see similarities in your thinking or actions. Whether you procrastinated, didn't set good boundaries, sought distraction with alcohol, food, or something else, the result is the same. You have faulty programming. Identifying what your true authentic-self desires and your hardwired preferences or values are will allow you to push past your preferred methods of sabotage when it shows up. We usually sabotage ourselves because deep down we don't feel worthy of living an extraordinary life or deserve the very best life has to offer.

My preferred methods of self-sabotage were drinking too much, not sticking to boundaries in relationships set by my values, and wanting someone to grow so much I became attached to the outcome. All of these distract me from my own purpose and lead to disappointment and regret. I'll talk more about distraction in a later section.

Choosing to not sabotage myself with drinking has left me feeling isolated and lonely at times. 99% of my friends use alcohol for connection so I am not included in many dinners or parties because I don't drink to get drunk anymore. When I do go I am no longer the life of party. I want to have friends and enjoy life, but prefer more deep and meaningful conversations. I also know how bad alcohol is for our brain. Since my mom's dementia I prefer to take as good of care of it as I can. I think many people are wound-up so tight they need alcohol to let go a little. I know in my heart God doesn't want us unconscious, which is what alcohol does. As I get older it takes two days to feel better if I drink so in order to stick to my goals I choose to abstain most of the time.

Once you determine who you really are and what away from values you want to grow through, monitoring self-sabotage daily will help you stay on track. Any behaviors or actions that aren't in alignment with your vision should be viewed as intruders. They only become a bad thing in your life if you take action on them so don't beat yourself up for just having the thoughts. For example, you might think about having something that is completely bad for you when you are trying to get healthy, but unless you eat it there is no self-sabotage.

You should identify for every goal or mindset attribute how you might sabotage yourself. For example, if you want a promotion, yet you are passive and lack self-worth you might sabotage yourself by not working hard or developing new skills. You fall into self-pity or are disappointed when other people get promoted. Expecting anything in life from others when you ultimately have all the power to make any of your dreams come true is a waste. I see this at my company all the time. People want leadership positions when they have never acted like a leader. They haven't mastered their own role, yet they believe they should be promoted simply because they desire it. A true leader doesn't need a title and is influential every day by pouring into people even when they aren't asked.

The most common way I see women sabotage themselves is with their daily disciplines. It is not big stuff – it is the little stuff. It starts with how little care they put into their physical and emotional health. Then it moves to subtle choices in their day that they eventually beat themselves up over. Why did I eat my son's left over chicken nuggets? Why didn't I go to the gym instead of visiting too long at Starbucks? Why didn't I make more sales calls at work and not take a long lunch? Avoidance, projection, and distraction appear to soothe us and before you know it years go by.

How does sabotage raise its ugly head for you? Do you vent and complain too much, focusing on negativity and not gratitude? Do you have difficulty managing your time and only take care of other people's needs instead of your own? Do you have fear but mask it with looking perfectly happy? Do you lack confidence but not take action towards your goals? Are you so busy you never slow down? Are you controlling and bossy?

These things will continue to manifest trying to pull you away from your Big Voice unless you are intentional about not letting them. I would suggest looking at all of your preferred methods of self-sabotage before you start your day so you are on guard against them. For example, if health is a big priority, yet you have a busy schedule, plan ahead to minimize the chance you will end up making an excuse that you have to get that Frappuccino and scone because there was nothing else. Trust me. I have been there. I ate at my desk for years and stuffed my face with whatever was around. Until I made the decision health was a priority, I fell victim to my excuses daily. Now I do food prep and plan for my schedule so I have lots of healthy options.

Even when we get clear on our goals and plans we need to accept we won't always be bursting with energy and passion. There will be seasons that we just need more rest and we aren't actually sabotaging ourselves. The minute I rewind choices and focus on them from a place of self-criticism and not curiosity, I make it worse. It is one thing to have an off day, but another thing to beat myself up for having an off day.

The only thing worse for me than lower energy is thinking about my low energy. My mind takes off into reasoning and leaves faith, acceptance, and self-compassion behind. I start hallucinating that I need to leave my job, take every technological device from my kids, never speak to my sister again, never want a relationship, and give up on my purpose.

It is crazy how fast this can happen if I give my Little Voice a tiny window to climb through. Even though I have still done my morning routine every day this year, I didn't have the level of energy I craved. How the f*!? did I get so hard on myself! It is seriously delusional that I can be healthy and purpose-driven 365 days a year! God even says we need to rest, but we don't. We still fill up seven days and live at a super-human pace. No wonder I am wiped out! I deserve to be and nothing is wrong with that.

We have to learn how to live and trust our bodies. We can't keep pushing ourselves to exhaustion and expect we won't burn out. We have to take the criticism lens off ourselves and simply become curious so we can awaken and surrender even further. If we can become joyfully dependent on God to guide us, life becomes magical. No longer do we need to push until we break and then build back up. We can stay consistent and accepting of our human constraints instead of expecting too much of ourselves. This people pleasing bullshit has gone on too long. It's time to get compassionate with ourselves. It's just too fricking ridiculous that we can do it all.

Where has this pressure come from? Who put it there? Why, if you now believe you have a choice, would you continue down that same path?

It's time to quit the downward spiral and make the necessary shift from self-criticism to curiosity. In my situation, I just needed to add up the uncertainty I had in my life to see I was overwhelmed. Since I needed more certainty I had to make new decisions and set new boundaries. I have also accepted not bursting out of bed at 5:30 a.m. doesn't mean anything is wrong. I see that my body needs more rest from the heightened level of energy I've been expending. I just needed to add more time alone to recharge. Once I identified my own "I am not enough" worry in my life I was able to commit to minimizing it.

We can attack ourselves from the inside out, even if things are going well. It is as if we are waiting for something bad to happen so we feel unsettled. This goes deep into whether we believe we are worthy or not. It can become fired-up if we are hormonal so calendar your month with your emotions. You might become aware of trends. If at certain times you are triggered more, become more intentional about not reacting.

Life is only as hard as you make it. If you remain attached that everything will become easy or you create unrealistic expectations for your life, or self then you will be disappointed. You need to learn how to overcome self-sabotage and have a plan ahead of time to ensure you stay in your Big Voice.

Away From Values

As I shared earlier, you need to identify your away from values and keep them in front of you. These are the values that show up but that no longer serve you. Even when you wake up and recognize where you need to go and grow, it doesn't end the suffering. Awareness will lead you to learn how to better react to triggers or emotions. This takes a massive willingness to sit with discomfort. I always wait on God to reveal His plan while I remain honest with myself and others. But it really sucks! It is honestly the worst ever for a Type-A driven woman to handle. The truth is, I still want all my worldly preferences to be met, yet I know this is not the path to true joy and peace.

Too many people see awareness or mindfulness as the destination when the truth is you are only beginning. Unwinding years of social programming and becoming confident again takes time. It is a long journey where your brain and thoughts are on fire. You will wonder who you are and be constantly reassessing who should be in your life and where you should be focusing your priorities.

I am blessed with complete self-awareness of my "away from values." Every morning I review them to keep me armed against them. As I face a day, I can attribute thoughts or emotions to them. These are my top away from values: perfectionism, self-pity, doubt, judgment, passivity, and fear of failure. It took years for me to isolate these and identify how they show up in my life.

Self-Pity is the funniest away from value in my life. My Big Voice knows that I live an incredibly blessed life but this shows up at the most random times for me. As my son and I cuddled on the couch (actually he was playing video games and I was across the room trying to talk to him), I was trying to connect with him. After a very gallant attempt, he turned to me and said "Mom...all I really want right now is for you to quit talking!". My first reaction was anger, then sadness, then self-pity. I didn't react at all and just said okay. I know that this is typical pre-teen behavior but I was sad. I felt alone and disconnected. I wondered what I had done to deserve this until miraculously I started to become grateful. I had always taught my kids to value honesty and the honest truth was he didn't feel like talking. Rather than pleasing me, he spoke his truth. My self-pity was replaced with celebration and I could laugh at how funny his comment was.

The doubt that I am exactly where I need to be, doing exactly what God wants me to be doing comes in when I finally stop for the day. It pops-up like an unwelcomed visitor annoying you when you least want it. Doubt asks questions about your parenting, relationships, and past sins and creates conflict within you. You should feel forgiven and confident, but doubt wants to steal that from you.

Judgment is what I am battling with most right now. We all have our unique lens as to how we see the world. When we expect others to see things the same way or don't accept them for their differences it is called judgment. It is never a good thing. Judgment can easily be blurred by wanting others to actualize their potential. When you see someone who has gifts and strengths but isn't using them, you may get triggered. Or perhaps someone is lazy and you are a hard worker. You have to get clear on accepting that each of us values things uniquely. What we value isn't right or wrong, just different. With our children we *MUST* push through this, accepting where they are without judgement. We can subtly help them to value certain things by valuing them ourselves. If they see us taking care of our health or working hard and being happy doing so, they might also value those things.

Trying to force our values on others who don't share them will only make us crazy. In relationships, I have fallen for someone's potential and not who they were being at that moment. This pattern has led me to judging them when they didn't live up to the standards I felt they could reach. It is a vicious cycle in my life that has led to relationships ending. I have also spent way too much time hallucinating and hypothesizing about the potential of the relationship or man, not the true reality of it.

The awareness required to know your non-negotiables is so critical in relationships. It's the only way you can accept and love all your differences and keep from falling victim to judgment. I am guilty of listening or seeing their behavior and formulating my own idea of what their values are versus having them tell me. Maybe a conversation early on made me classify them as growth-minded based on what I per-ceived as their personality type. Then the evidence of how they have been living, with a job they don't like and minimal financial security shows me the opposite is true. We all fantasize about an ideal partner. If you find yourself judging someone, your reality may be blurred. You may expect too much of your partner; a standard they can't live up to.

Passivity is another big one for me. When I worry about others' opinions or get overwhelmed I can become passive. I don't stand up for what I believe and have a hard time taking action or communicating my needs. It normally shows up as wanting to run or retreat. It feels like pulling back instead of pushing forward. I have worked very hard on passivity and the result is that it appears less and less in my life.

The downside of being so intentional about passivity is I see it much more in others which can lead me to judgment. Accepting as humans we all do different things when we have limitations or barriers to push through releases some of this judgment. When stressed, men tend to become passive, whereas women tend to become more controlling. I set goals that are the opposite of being passive so that I approach each day like it's my last. The fear of my mom's condition being genetic pushes me daily to never take life for granted.

Fear of failure shows up for me mainly in parenting and relationships. I am blessed that my professional confidence is high since my parenting and relationship confidence are not. Having had a failed marriage, I am constantly plagued with the fear of failure in choosing the wrong life partner. My pattern has been to choose a slightly different version of my ex-husband. I accept I am someone that likes a "fixer-upper," but then I eventually "flip" them when the relationship requires more energy than I can tolerate.

In parenting, I worry my divorce or who I am will negatively affect my kids. I often am so intentional that I am not real or present. I have set standards and expectations that could be unrealistic for my kids to achieve. I have to be mindful about unconditionally loving and accepting them. My daughter triggers old wounds from my divorce because she is a lot like her dad. She will cut off love and emotion for unknown reasons and then I spend time trying to figure her out. I ask her the dreaded question too often which is "what is wrong?" just like I did with her dad. It always makes things worse. I want so badly for her to respect me and value love and kindness the way I do, but I know we aren't the same. I have had to accept nothing is wrong she just doesn't feel like being connected at that moment. It is easier for me to parent my son because he is completely like me and outward with his emotions and triggers. My fear shows up when I worry I am not enough. I focus daily on reminding myself it is impossible for me to fail if I love and accept them unconditionally.

Once you isolate your top away from values, self-awareness can lead you to creating new behaviors and emotions. Your away from values are buried deep though so just be armed against them and prepare at times to be uncomfortable.

> *"The distance is nothing; it is only the first step that is difficult."* Mme. du Deffand

LIVING A BIG VOICE LIFE

"Your teacher can open the door, but you must enter yourself." Chinese Proverb

Now that you have a solid plan that allows your Big Voice to guide you to live an amazing life, it's time to delve into executing. How do you stay in your Big Voice and continue to let it rise even as your Little Voice is screaming for attention? What can you do that will help?

The first thing you learned is to begin to think differently and be more selective about what you do with certain thoughts to cultivate more mindfulness. This is TMS, your Thought Management Strategy. The second thing you learned to do is clarify your priorities, create your vision, and then define your goals. After that you learned strategies to reduce triggers, self-sabotage, and away from values so you stay on course. In this last section, I will review things you encounter in life that, with intention, become easier to handle i.e. managing your energy levels, accepting your capacity, making decisions, managing stress, letting go, putting love first, forgiving and loving yourself and others, balancing your life, walking through pain and shame, parenting, and navigating your hormones.

Managing Your Energy

Let's start with energy. Many women feel they just don't have the energy that joyful or balanced women do. They believe they should jump out of bed with energy and then overthink why they don't. Brendan Burchard, a motivational speaker and author, has in my opinion the best metaphor for describing energy. He refers to it as a power plant. A power plant has no energy to begin. It must be generated. The same is true of us.

After I let his words sink in, I began to recall that many times when I had self-pity I had lower energy. I also realized that towards the end of the day when my kids needed me most I had lower energy. I blamed the weather, how hard my kid's schedule was, the magnitude of work projects, etc. I had forgotten I was completely responsible for my own energy. I had always been described as a high-energy person, but I realized this didn't necessarily hold throughout the day. I recognized I needed to be more intentional about how much joy I showed up with. My kids are higher on my priority list than work but work was getting all my energy.

Rather than beat myself up, I took this nugget and set new intentions. I vowed that before I went into any meeting I would set the intention for it and prepare my state more. Even just two minutes to visualize the impact would help. I also made a commitment to bring more energy and joy home after work. I would ask more questions and weave our values into their life experiences. For example, if they were acting entitled, instead of telling them to be more grateful and getting mad, I'd let them discover gratitude through the questions I would ask.

There are days or seasons where waking up and staying committed to your goals and disciplines are ridiculously hard. You may be struggling with a decision or under stress. Your physical body cannot handle as much as your emotionally developed self. It is easy to start beating yourself up for being lazy or fatigued. This will not help but will only make it worse.

You have grown so much in your ability to manage your thoughts and emotions. You are committed to joy in spite of your circumstances, yet you have low energy and because of it you are struggling. This might be a cue that you need to "let go" of something or you need to reevaluate your vision.

If you experience lower energy in your life, just analyze if you are carrying anything heavy. If you are, it will weigh you down. It can happen when you are not having enough fun or not being adventurous. We all need something to look forward to. We can become too disciplined which may help us accomplish our goals but then leave us feeling bored. I actually have to keep on my goals that I will have more fun weekly to ensure that this is always a focus. I know for most they have too much fun and not enough discipline, but it is finding the right balance that really brings you more joy and energy.

Some other intentions you should make if you want to increase energy are to exercise at least five days a week and eat healthy. I am not going to go into this in depth. There are so many choices for how to accomplish this that I'll leave it to you to decide what works best. We all love different activities. I love yoga, walking, hiking, and doing a quick strength training circuit at home. You might love running, the gym, or tennis. Even if you say you hate exercise try everything because you will eventually find something you like. One day you will love the energy it brings you.

Managing our energy and state becomes easier if we make it a top priority. If you aren't intentional about cultivating energy and reinforcing your Big Voice, you will not feel as much joy as you could. Too many women feel exhausted, depressed, overwhelmed, unfulfilled, hopeless, etc. yet they don't have a plan to change; one that they execute on a daily basis. Going to a therapy session once a week when you don't have a clear plan will never work. Talking about how you feel and getting another perspective will help, but you won't see lasting change without a solid commitment to manage your state and energy level.

Just starting with two simple tweaks will help and then you can layer on additional aspects. First, your vocabulary has to change. Using new words to describe how you feel will cultivate change. Instead of complaining or using words like good or okay, switch this to amazing, extraordinary, fabulous, etc. when people ask how you are. Second, you need to minimize sharing your problems because sharing them only reemphasizes the negativity. If you must share, share with someone who can lead you back to your intention for more joy. You also need to determine if you are an introvert or extrovert. The difference isn't who likes to socialize more but how you generate energy. I had no idea I was actually an introvert and needed a lot of alone time to recharge. You may find you have been unintentionally draining yourself because your social calendar is too full.

Accepting Your Capacity

For some unknown reason we all have a different level of capacity. Some people can handle a lot of priorities and other people shut down with just a few. The saying God only gives us what we can handle seems like bullshit to me. I've seen how some women simply can't handle their lives and live with depression or anxiety. They turn to doctors as if they have a medical problem when the truth is they have too much on their plates or minds. They believe their unhappiness or feeling of overwhelm can be cured by altering their brain chemistry whereas the truth is they just haven't dedicated any time to writing a new story.

If I felt burdened or out of whack every day, I could understand why someone would seek help. However, this epidemic is causing more problems than you can imagine. Most medications have side effects that impact the overall quality of someone's life and can often deaden their ability to feel. If you think about it the doctor prescribing the medicine is often not the one responsible for therapy and no one really gets to the root cause of the issue. I know there are women out there that truly do suffer from mental illness, but the rise in prescription medication is a good indicator we are over-medicating a problem we could deal with in a different manner. The ability to feel is what makes us human and alive. Hopefully more women turn to therapy or seek the tools that can help them where medication won't.

I want you to consider that all of this suffering may be caused by not living truthfully. Maybe you aren't happy in your marriage or your job or hate staying at home. The more you bottle up your truth the more depressed and anxious you will become. I believe you have optimum capacity when you are aligned with your truth and purpose. When you have a vision for your life and work hard towards your goals, you have more energy.

Capacity is both emotional and physical. There are so many stressful jobs or ways to serve that require a high level of emotional intelligence. If you are someone that takes on other people's problems, you have to be careful about which jobs you choose. Don't ever judge yourself for not being on the frontlines of pressure. Accepting yourself for who you are and recognizing you have an individual purpose is half the battle. Physically, we all have different capacity levels as well. Some people get fatigued with a full plate and others don't. You cannot expect to run a marathon on the first day, so just build up to having more. Sleep, stress management, and what you eat all play into your physical capacity.

If you are in a relationship or are a parent, you do have to make sacrifices, but you must still have a plan to take care of yourself. If your only purpose is being a wife or mom, you will eventually burn out and one day wake up feeling empty. You have to feed your own soul as well.

Making Big Decisions

In life, we are often presented with big decisions around which we may, or may not, have clarity. Our desire for certainty or control often leads us to try and make these decisions too quickly. We think repeatedly about potential outcomes or how we got to this place. We may work ourselves into a state of anxiety or fear. Our belief is that all the pressure is on us and that this decision is far more important than it really is.

If you are clear that life will unfold exactly as it needs to, you will have a deep sense of peace. It will feel like God or the Universe has guided you and there is really no other choice. You will feel like you don't need to overthink the situation. It doesn't matter if the decision is right or wrong; ultimately you know it is the decision you need to make right now.

If you lack clarity, you will probably spin yourself out trying to seek it until you adopt a new perspective. There is another way. If you see yourself as a decisive person you may want to try this because you may have been making decisions too quickly; not fully letting God or the Universe help you. If you felt pressure and anxiety about the decisions you made it is a sure sign this is the case. Even though you had clarity, you were still hypothesizing like crazy if the decision was the right one. The new way involves trust, deep intuition, awareness, and patience. You must begin to trust the idea that life happens for you. You must trust God and the Universe will work to help things become clear.

You must seek to understand the deep intuition that is connected to both your emotional and physical being. Your body will help you know right from wrong. If you have a sick feeling about something you are facing, listen to it. Your deep intuition will speak to you through thoughts that are clear and precise. It doesn't speak of the past or future. It only provides awareness. It doesn't have fear or doubt. Deep intuition comes when you are present and free of thought. Clearing your mind of the pressure to make a decision will call deep intuition to appear.

Awareness of your thinking and role will help. As your mind races to try and figure things out like a puzzle, you will be able to remind yourself to be still and patient. You can use your TMS strategy to sort your thoughts and only allow your Big Voice thoughts to guide you. Your awareness will be the voice of reason in your life so that you can be patient.

Being patient isn't easy for any of us. We have been taught that part of our value in life is to make quick decisions. We have seen that risk takers and leaders who are decisive are the ones who prosper and succeed. We don't see the people who are patient who have succeeded because most likely they haven't shared their story. They are too humble or they avoid the spotlight intentionally.

Patience comes from trust and acceptance that life will guide us to have the deep intuition we require to make decisions when we need to. Patience may override artificial deadlines if we aren't ready to make a decision. It trusts if we are not ready that everything will unfold in due time. Maintaining patience means you must be strong enough to quiet your urge to force things. You must let go of the idea that your value is to be decisive and realize sometimes not making a decision is the best decision. You must let go of the false idea you are only strong if you have clarity. You must accept that it is okay to be in a position where you don't know what to do.

Your Big Voice and most authentic self must start looking at decisions differently. You are faced with little and big decisions every day that take far too much of your time and energy. Additionally, many of your decisions are already made for you because you have deeply entrenched habits that switch you to autopilot. Look at a typical day and figure out what you can do differently to make good behaviors like exercise or self-care a habit so you can have the energy for bigger decisions. You can release your anxiety, fear, and worry by trusting life will happen for you. Things will occur that will guide you and you can quit hypothesizing. Your Big Voice will show up and help you push past your Little Voice and its desire to derail you. You just have to be patient and willing to be uncomfortable with not trying to figure things out. Remember we cannot predict the future, just think critically about whatever you need to decide and move on.

You must start trying to live differently or nothing will change. You will only bring on more suffering when you are faced with big decisions. Once you know what you want, you can set a goal for clarity, but don't have any attachment to it. Then sit back and watch life start unfolding for you. Once you do make a decision, remain committed to it no matter what happens. You will grow and have gratitude. There are no wrong decisions, even if it turns out differently than you want. All decisions, both good and bad, eventually come together to create the life you are supposed to be living.

One Buddhist monk leaned over to another and quietly asked, "Are you not thinking what I'm not thinking?"

Stress Management

Another area that is critical to having balance, improving your health, and reducing suffering is to learn to manage your stress. Stress generally arises from two things:

1. Trying to control things that are beyond your reach, power, or authority and/or

2. A scarcity mindset

Let's talk about wanting to have control over everything first. We think that if we have control we will have certainty. But that's simply not true. It's the very uncertain nature of life that causes us stress. We can't tolerate that so many things are out of our hands.

The biggest aha for me was in understanding that we, as women, lack balance when it comes to being empathetic. The problems of all the people in our circle of influence become our problems. We often care too much. This causes us to have a 24/7 mentality. We feel like we always have to be available and that is devastating to our stress levels.

What you need to do is set boundaries. It changed my world for the better when I became more disciplined about setting and maintaining boundaries. My stress declined to almost nothing. You have to let the Universe do its work and not take on the expectations of others. You must accept uncertainty and look forward to the infinite choices it will open up for you. Take a step back and say, "I don't need to take this home with me. I don't need to carry these things. I don't need to take on the stress and be weighed down with the issues of my friends and family."

I think Deepak Chopra says it best in his Law of Detachment:

"In detachment lies the wisdom of uncertainty . . . in the wisdom of uncertainty lies the freedom from our past, from the known, which is the prison of past conditioning. And in our willingness to step into the unknown, the field of all possibilities, we surrender

ourselves to the creative mind that orchestrates the dance of the universe."

One of the boundaries I have put in place for myself, and one that has had a profound impact on how I set myself up for a successful day, is to not check my email before 8 a.m. or after 8 p.m. You may not be aware but email is a major stress producer. A study by Professor Tom Jackson, from Loughborough University, showed 92% of the participants had elevated blood pressure and heart rates when checking their email. This is generally caused by email that is wasting our time or by email that we feel requires an immediate response. Other studies have shown that people are less productive for the rest of the day if they check their email within 60 minutes of waking up.

I strongly suggest that you review your priorities and goals for the day instead. Focus on your I AM statements so you can step into the person you want to be for the day rather than checking email. Your value proposition should be to show up as the best "you" every day, not to always answer the phone or be available 24/7.

The second big stressor for women is a scarcity mindset. I can't emphasize enough how destructive this mindset is to your sustainable success. You'll know you're in a scarcity mindset if you hear yourself saying things like: "I just don't know where I'm going to get in my career. I don't know how I'm going to make a living. I don't know if I'm doing the right activities." A lack of clarity is what I've found to be the major contributor to a scarcity mindset. Not enough clarity in your life plan. Not enough clarity around the things you need to do every day in order to be successful. This stress can paralyze you. It keeps you from taking risks and creating opportunities.

From a practical standpoint what can you do to reduce stress? Try these three things:

1. Become aware of your triggers and use the Trigger Management System. Which of your preferences that aren't being met cause a trigger that makes you anxious, nervous, and stressed? Again, the better we learn to manage our triggers, to put space between reacting and responding, the less stress we'll have. A great way to create space, when you can't write in your journal, is to breathe. Plant your feet firmly on the ground with your legs uncrossed. Take a deep breath in through your nose then let it out through your mouth. If you do this about three times, you'll feel your body relax allowing you to use the space to manage your trigger.

2. Create better disciplines. Put disciplines and boundaries in place so you can run your own day and not let other people's priorities run it for you.

It would be nice to be motivated every day but we know discipline is what really matters. Leave time in your day so that you can win it by being proactive about what you accomplish. Regardless of the problems that come along, you've won your day if you took action towards your purpose, vision, or goals and stayed in alignment with your priorities.

3. Be mindful of how you take care of yourself. To live an amazing life you have to have an abundance of energy. You won't have the energy you need unless you're healthy. If you don't take care of yourself, eating right, drinking water, reducing stress, and exercising regularly then you simply won't have the energy you need to deal with the inevitable situations that will arise.

What you don't want is to let the emotions or thoughts that are triggered to cause stress that will undermine your ability to stay disciplined. While you can't stop thoughts or emotions, you can stop the suffering by better controlling your actions and feelings. It is often the underdeveloped side of our ego, our lower selves, trying to make us feel important that causes stress. It pushes us to connect with people by complaining; it pushes us to connect with people by feeling stressed out. We almost feel like it's our responsibility i.e. if I'm going to make a ton of money then I'd better be stressed out doing it.

You have to let go of the idea that stress is a good thing. There is nothing good about it. Pushing ourselves and working hard is good but that should not be confused with stress. Your Little Voice will cause you to distract yourself and then beat yourself up over it. We cannot run from pressure but we can change how we deal with it. If stress is a huge part of your life, I would urge you to seek help immediately to minimize the devastating affects it will have on your emotional and physical well-being.

Managing Disappointment

Have you ever had one of those seasons where no matter how hard you try someone is disappointed in you or you just feel like everyone is? Or you are disappointed in yourself? The truth is you cannot avoid thoughts like this if you have had them before, but you can avoid the self-pity or feeling hopeless to please everyone. I don't know where we acquired the false belief that we could please everyone or that people will always be loyal, even if you have poured into them. Shifting this core belief and learning not to take things personally will release you from a tremendous amount of suffering. It doesn't happen overnight. You will need several real-life experiences to practice the belief of not needing to please everyone.

I have had a handful of these opportunities recently. A series of disappointments in other people stacked up quickly at home and at work. Although I tried to rise above them, my Little Voice started to create self-loathing thoughts that suggested I quit my job, rid myself of stress, take 100 percent control over my kid's educational path, and accept that unless I did something drastic things would be hopeless for us all. I started to lose my power and feel sorry for myself.

I was feeling this way one evening when my kids and I were chatting after dinner. We had just sold our old home and they were talking about how they missed it. They went into details of what they missed and then what they wanted if we were to buy a new home. The guilt of pulling them from their childhood home that had every imaginable thing a kid could want was heavy. I had moved them into a modest rental that was much closer to work and school in addition to being better for me financially, but I still felt bad. My son threw in that I should have never divorced their dad; nothing had been the same since. I took a moment after hearing this to just breathe. I realized that he could only process what had happened through his own perception. The old house was more convenient for him, it was bigger and he liked the set-up. It was his desire for easier, bigger, and better that drove his views. My daughter chimed-in that she understood her dad and I weren't compatible, but quickly followed that up with she wanted us to get a modern farmhouse which included a living area of her own. They had zero understanding that their comments or desires were creating an internal disruption for me as I felt pressure to keep their life the same as it was before the divorce.

It was to them, an innocent conversation. They had no idea how hard it had been for me alone to financially maintain that home for the last five years. They also had no idea how much guilt I had to process after the divorce. I could have made a decision to stay for them, but then would have been miserable personally. If you put your own physical and emotional health first you will not please everyone. Rather than feeling bad about yourself every time that you disappoint others, you have to get stronger and more powerful internally. Even for the biggest voices this takes constant intention and effort.

If you work, or are involved in any group that requires collaboration or dependence on others, it is impossible to avoid conflict or disappointment even if you do everything right. People have their own opinions and often will do what is best for them regardless of what you have done for them. When this happens, it is hard to remain detached and unscathed emotionally. Humans are imperfect and they can only see most situations through their own eyes. Depending on their development level, they may project their issues on you. If you see it and feel it, know you cannot win a battle against someone else's ego.

Years ago a friend of mine who I had been supporting at work left the company for what she considered a better opportunity. She was not happy with the new leadership in our company and didn't feel a part of our culture. In addition she still had feelings of abandonment by a previous manager who left years before. I knew this and tried to support her even more. At the time though, I felt nothing I did was ever enough. I knew unless she made the decision to change her mindset, she was in a downward spiral with us. It appeared she was only focusing on the negative and not the positive.

Had I spent more time understanding her perception, I could have been more empathetic. Instead, I was so focused on everything we did for her that I deemed the whole situation hopeless. The truth is she was suffering. Looking back, she needed a change and I should have supported that instead of trying to force something that wasn't right.

During her departure, I shared my opinions with her about who she was being at work and what she could have done differently. I immediately knew after I said it, that I was having a conversation with her ego and not her. It was not the right time. She wanted my blessing; not my opinions. I took her resignation personally and not professionally. I wanted so badly for her to see her suffering was a choice and that she could rise above it, but it was not the right time or place. I was hurt by her dissatisfaction with the company instead of remaining detached.

In the mortgage industry where I work it is so easy to get spun out because you have recruiters calling you every day telling you how much better another company is and how much more money you will make. Sales people are recruited and rarely ever apply for jobs. I lost my ability to relate to how she was feeling and stepped into my own self-pity feeling of not enough. The truth is I do pour into people that work for me and build the false expectation they should be loyal. Unintentionally this only leads to pain long-term and my own suffering. You must accept others for who they are and limit the opinions that you share unless they ask for them.

This feeling of not enough may pop up in many areas of your life. We spread ourselves so thin it is often impossible to be really good at any one thing. As you discover your true priorities it is important that you keep an eye on your "I AM Enough" belief and mindset. Making the decision to believe this in spite of life's challenges or disruptions will help you stay centered. I actually have "I Am Enough" on my list to remind myself every morning there is nothing not enough about me.

There is absolutely no value in believing you are not enough and being disappointed in yourself. When and if you get stuck in this pattern, quickly have a plan to reset yourself. I remember as a young child being scared I would step in quicksand after watching an episode of Gilligan's Island. The scene is actually a great metaphor for dealing with that sinking feeling. Although Gilligan is trying to find a vine to save the Captain, only the Captain has the ability to pull himself out. We all want to be rescued or saved when we are suffering, but accepting that we are the only ones (with God's help) who can pull ourselves out will help us be more decisive and clear when it happens.

It also helps to understand and believe this when we see someone else suffering. They are the ones with the power to pull them out. You might have the knowledge and wisdom, but I wouldn't share it, unless they have decided it's something they want. It takes effort to hold back, but trust that will always be the best decision. You will constantly be disappointed trying to help others and expecting them to grow when they aren't ready to do so.

Choosing to believe "I Am Enough" and reminding yourself daily will minimize your faulty programming. One core aspect of this is to accept yourself wholeheartedly in this moment, but still maintain a future vision of who you want to become. If you focus on who you want to become too much you will never feel like you are enough. It is a delicate balance that you will need to practice until it feels right.

You are the only one who can feel enough. This requires zero external opinions or perceptions from others. All external situations or circumstances are happening for you. Perfectionists find this takes more work. Even if you let others down you have to maintain the belief that you are enough. Be strong so you can overcome deeply patterned thoughts and emotions. Keep yourself in constant love and acceptance even when you screw up or other people project their disappointment or frustration towards you. We need to learn to accept criticism through an opportunity lens rather than from a "not enough" belief. Feeling disappointment from others or yourself will steal your joy but only if you allow it to.

Distractions

Once you have awareness you will more easily be able to spot self-sabotaging thoughts and emotions. Since you created your life vision and goals, you are able to differentiate behavior or actions that lead you closer to or farther away from them. The things that draw you farther away usually happen when you aren't feeling strong. Maybe something has gone wrong or achieving your goals is harder than you thought so you feel you need a distraction. I have found in my life distractions also happen when I am not 100 percent clear about a goal. Clarity is a requirement in order for you to remain focused and committed.

People often don't achieve their goals or live the life they envision because they sabotage themselves or allow problems to derail them. Then they allow distractions to take the place of what they should be doing. You may have the best intentions and as long as everything is perfect you stay on track. When things aren't perfect and something disrupts your progress, you can fall back into old patterns.

My health goals include exercising and eating healthy. I also have goals to do yoga or meditate a couple of times a week. Although I am clear about how I want to feel, if I am tired and out of balance I sabotage myself. The minute another option presents itself I say yes. I easily make excuses and give myself permission to slack off. It becomes harder every day to get back to my routine even though I thrive in it.

For example, having my nieces in my home for over a week last summer disrupted my schedule. I had been caring for them instead of being able to exercise when I wanted. The truth is I could have done it, but I would have needed to wake up earlier or do it later. Rather than making some adjustments, I just didn't do anything. In this situation, I have options: get committed and start today, give myself permission to take a break because of my schedule, or beat myself up that I am sabotaging myself.

Thoughts that I will not stay in shape or look good in a bathing suit have crept in as well as thoughts I won't remain mentally strong if I don't take care of my body. Being aware that I need to love, accept, and forgive myself above all else overpowers those thoughts. I accepted that I had become distracted and could not be perfect. However, I knew I needed to recommit to my goals.

Another area women often distract themselves is seeking attention from someone they are attracted to but is bad for them. Whether you are in a committed relationship or not, getting attention from someone you like can make you feel alive. There is nothing wrong with harmless flirtation, but crossing the line may happen quickly. We all want to feel needed and adored. We want to be captivating to someone. The challenge is that this euphoric feeling is hard to sustain in a committed relationship. You may get bored and be taken off-guard if someone shows interest in you. You will sabotage your relationship if you allow this to happen. You have to be alert if you have a history of this. Renewing your relationship goals and remaining grateful to your partner will help. Also setting boundaries in these friendships is vital. Make a decision that you will not spend any time alone with the person or drink around them. You cannot be critical of yourself for liking the attention or anticipation that communicating with them brings. However, you can learn from it and remind yourself nothing external can ever fill you. Use this experience to grow even deeper so it happens less and less.

There are seasons where you are under so much stress or pressure that you simply cannot handle another thing. Your brain will fall victim to distractions when this happens to disrupt the state you are in. The ego can become stronger if your Big Voice is weak. Taking on too much will eventually shut you down.

One of my favorite Bible stories is when Jesus goes to Martha's house. Her sister Mary sits at Jesus's feet and listens intently. Martha is busy taking care of other things and asks Jesus if it is wrong that Mary can sit there while she is the one doing everything. He makes it clear Mary is the one that is doing what is right by being present and not busy. We have to slow down, especially when we have a major crisis in our lives or we will sabotage ourselves. We also need to be prepared for them by taking care of ourselves throughout life. If you aren't feeding your soul and strengthening your Big Voice it will be that much harder if a storm hits.

Forcing yourself to find gratitude in every day and even every tragedy will help get you through. Your natural defense system is faulty and will lead you down the wrong path. As twisted as it sounds based on everything you've learned, you CAN get your needs met by complaining or feeling sorry for yourself. We all have some desire to be significant so we have to be cautious.

Once you are aware enough to see yourself

becoming distracted, you should also praise your humanness. No matter how strong you are, there are still maximum capacity levels that you can endure. Some things are too much to handle on your own. Without my faith and commitment to prayer, I know I would have shut down completely or sabotaged my goals long ago. Surrendering when you are at your capacity is the only way to maintain joy. Even though you might want control, you need to learn how to let go.

Letting Go

"Nothing in the universe can stop you from letting go and starting over . . ." Guy Finley

We crave control in life so that we have more certainty and assurance that everything will be okay. Yet the act of trying to maintain control will make you suffer internally. We worry, we hypothesize, we tell others what to do, and we are disappointed when it seems no one can meet our expectations. Nothing good comes from trying to control our life even though temporarily it makes us feel better.

We cannot be controlling and present at the same time. It is impossible to experience true joy and surrender and try to control things simultaneously. You must learn to let go and become more trusting that life happens for you.

I suspect when we had too much uncertainty in our lives growing up, we needed to find some area that was more predictable. We then chose something we had power over to start controlling such as our health, a relationship, socializing, or school. We became obsessed with it as it fed the part of our human need for certainty. Our life may have appeared stable or happy on the outside, but inside we were in turmoil. As I've told you before, my personal struggle has been with perfectionism. I cared more about the perception of others than figuring out what really made me happy. Any decision or situation was not faced with my own authentic excitement, but with how I could gain more significance and attention.

As women we tend to seek control when at a deep level we are simply insecure. There was a time I didn't believe I was a unique masterpiece. I questioned my importance in this world and didn't love myself fully. I worried when I walked into a room what others were thinking about me. I kept myself distracted if I was uncomfortable. I lacked the tools needed to see what I was doing to myself. I didn't know I was causing my own suffering.

The only way we can be free is to let go of

control. It is the most important part of our healing process. If you have been controlling your whole life, this process requires your willingness to do this. You will be unwinding years of repetitive thinking pathways and attachments. Letting go does not mean you lack having a vision or goals, but releasing yourself from the attachment to the results. You will begin to enjoy the journey instead of requiring more to happen before you become happy. You can let go of the false idea that you are responsible for how everything turns out. You also accept life happens for you so any setbacks are celebrated as new opportunities to grow.

If you look back at all your controlling ways you will see they didn't result in joy, peace, or more love. They caused you pain. The long list of "if onlys" haunted your thoughts and emotions. If only my partner changed or did X, Y, Z. If only my boss valued me. If only my body was perfect. If only my kids would conform. All these fantasies you want control over will never happen. The only choice you really have is to commit to being happy right now in spite of everything not being exactly as you want.

All of it really doesn't matter anyway. If you had everything in your control you would find something else to move on to. The thoughts and anxiety that our desire for control creates is habitual. If you think back to your desire to control your body at an early age, you dieted or focused on it. You may have even reached your desired weight or look, but then what? You got nothing but an empty celebration and then moved on. You are likely still doing the same thing today about the same issue. Letting go would require you shift from wanting to control what you look like to I want to feel healthy. You eat well and exercise. You don't focus on it. You simply love your body every day. Trust me, it feels so much better. I can still have impostor or Little Voice thoughts come and say things like, "Your stomach isn't flat enough," but now my Big Voice quickly dismisses that nonsense. We all know at some level that it is what's on the inside that counts, but we can forget this as we try and exert control.

The day I decided I would no longer fight my sister's battles was sad and scary. After 30 years of trying to help and save her, I finally made a decision to let go. I had to accept she had brought three beautiful children into this world and either she, or their father, was the one responsible for their well-being. Her lack of follow through in getting help and support has created the mess she is in.. I will no longer financially support or enable her when she doesn't seek help. I think on some level my sister's pain was a distraction to me in living my best life. I also think I did it out of guilt because I felt bad life seemed easier for me. Countless hours and restless nights spent in worrying or hypothesizing what I should do next were wasted. Watching her make poor choices or avoid getting things done caused me so much stress. I was in a state of fight or flight when she was in a bad place. My body became fatigued and I felt helpless. I had to let go once and for all that I needed to save her. It wasn't easy; I'd made the same promise and slipped before. This time though I knew in my heart I could no longer live this way especially since everything is now in the court's hands.

So how do you let go? The first step is making it a goal. Then from there you can start to see how many opportunities you have to practice your new decision. Become aware of your thoughts before you respond or react to any situation. Giving life the space it needs to unfold and watching it all as a spectator versus a player will help you make better decisions. I am not suggesting you don't need to take action towards your vision, goals, or plans, you just don't have to stress or assimilate so much.

Letting go takes years of practice. Starting today will set you on your journey to true freedom. You will be disappointed and anxious less and leave more room for adventure and trust. Once you know what you want, trusting God and the universe to orchestrate everything for you will release pressure you may have been carrying forever.

Forgiveness

The process of forgiving yourself and others is a necessary step to becoming your best self. Not only do you need to let go of anything you have stored as pain from your past, you also need to know how to do it on a regular basis. Once you learn how, you will release much stress and anger from your life.

The past and all your wounds are there with or without you knowing. Events or emotions have been stored and will give your ego direction so that it avoids similar situations. Your heart can become closed as well. Nothing good comes from holding resentment or blame inside of you.

Looking at the past can hurt for many people. You may have been a victim of abuse or not have felt loved. You may have been abandoned or made several bad choices. You may have lost loved ones or had failed relationships. There is no one who has escaped painful life experiences. The difference is how each person dealt with them.

Avoidance is easier for many. Maybe you emotionally shut down and powered through. Maybe you turned to external vices like food, alcohol, drugs, shopping, or men. The common theme from the past was this is too painful to deal with so I am not going to deal with it consciously.

Picture a storage unit full of boxes that contain hurtful memories. They might be divided into names or seasons in your life. Each box has stored emotions or pain that you need to eliminate. Each one is linked to someone you need to forgive. It could be God because you felt He did not protect you, it could be you for making terrible choices, or it could be people like your parents or significant others.

Just like it is not possible to open all the boxes at the same time, you can't forgive everyone and everything at the same time. You cannot expect to release all resentment or blame overnight. You can only make a decision to start. Similar to releasing pain, you have to find the positive aspects of all this resentment or blame. Find one thing to be grateful for as you forgive those who have harmed you. At the beginning, you might not be able to do this. I worked with a woman recently whose birth father abandoned her. She had immense feelings of anger and sadness that he had chosen not to try with her. As we began the forgiveness process, she could only thank him for bringing her to life. Over time the list of things she could be grateful to him for grew. It eventually led her to understanding her father wasn't competent to love her the way she desired. As she forgave him for making a choice to give her up, she also thanked him for the closeness she had with her mom and all the life experiences his absence created.

If you have a long list of stored resentment or blame, I would suggest starting a forgiveness journal. Dedicate a page or two to each person or event that holds an emotional wound. This is an opportunity to purge out every thought you ever had, whether positive or negative. Then over time, you can pick it up and work through each one.

Sometimes guilt can stop you from forgiving. It is important to realize no one is perfect and even the greatest of parents need forgiveness. I see individuals idolize a parent for doing it all or raising them on their own while they know in their heart their parent was the cause of much of their suffering. Because they believe their parent sacrificed so much, they are afraid to admit they weren't a strong role model. Any feeling you had growing up or now that is slightly "blame-ish," remove it. You no longer want any of that toxic thinking in your body. You cannot be truly authentic if you have stored any blame.

This process of eliminating blame and guilt may need to be guided by a therapist or healer if you were a victim of emotional, sexual, or physical abuse. Trusting your Creator will hold that person accountable will help you forgive. Although this person or persons made evil choices, you have no idea what pain or anger caused them to do it. You often hear, "But they had a choice." Did they? Addictions control people. Minds can be overtaken by evil thoughts. The person God brought into this world may not even have any power anymore. As hard as forgiveness sounds, it opens your heart to a whole new realm of possibilities. You don't even have to tell this person you forgive them, you just need to let the stored emotions of blame for your life go.

I recognize that my sister and I are not at all alike. Although raised by the same parents, we had different personalities and parenting. I will never figure out why she chose suffering for so many years. I have to eliminate the idea though that my choices and life are good and her choices and life are bad. Maintaining the idea that my way is better only leads to pain. I forgive my sister often for all the drama and volatility she creates for me and our family, but I also accept some of it is out of her control. She simply doesn't have the tools or commitment to change.

Every day I have to be armed against my triggers and aware that old wounds try and guide me. I can feel frustration result in "always" and "never" feelings and I start to blame others if I am losing my joy. Tony Robbins has a philosophy that if you are going to blame people for the bad, you have to blame them for the good too. The process of forgiveness opens up an analysis of how problems or people actually have affected the direction of your life. So many negative events or seasons have made us stronger. You may have hit bottom in a relationship or in addiction, but then arose from it a much better version of yourself.

As I journal on forgiveness, I remember to find gratitude in the process. I forgive myself through-out the process as well, that I either wasn't awake or wasn't ready to face whatever trigger or situa-tion arose that I now need to forgive someone for. Forgiveness is more about giving a gift to you and releasing stored pain than it is about giving a gift to someone else. It's not important that you share the forgiveness. You can forgive someone and still choose to not have contact with them. I pray even more for those I know who are narcissistic and not good people. Releasing yourself from anything you have been carrying frees up your heart. Picture a tight belt or shield around your heart loosening. That's how it feels when you let go and forgive.

Your ability to have self-compassion and quickly forgive when you make mistakes will release you from avoidable suffering. I recently went through this over some parenting issues. I had a great deal of pain and regret for the pressure my daughter felt to be perfect. I blamed myself that I unintentionally set the bar so high by how I was living that she was waiting to fail and felt like she would never be enough. Although I told her daily I loved her unconditionally and that she was amazing, she feared disappointing me. I had been so intentional about raising strong and kind kids I crossed the pendulum of being real. I was mad at myself for things I said or did or how I compared my life to theirs as if I expected them to avoid the mistakes I made.

My daughter and I are working through the anxiety it caused and I have had to work through forgiving myself quickly in order to move on. I was sad and worried before I made a decision to just let it go and forgive myself for anything I may have done wrong. I found gratitude in the situation (nothing bad had happened – we may become closer than ever – we have access to tremendous resources, etc.) and accepted this was simply another level of surrender I needed to reach.

As I was working through forgiving myself, I

came across even more areas in my life where I had open wounds. I did a comparison between my daughter and my 13-year-old self while thinking of all I had to be grateful for in our relationship. All I can say is WOW! She is so much more mature and grounded than I ever was. She doesn't seek significance in the way I did, nor has she made bad decisions with alcohol or boys. Although the exercise was to find gratitude in our current situation, it became more than that. I found I had a lot of forgiving of myself to do. All I ever wanted is for my kids to not make the mistakes I made and not veer too far away from God. What I really uncovered is I wanted them to be perfect. So I passed on my craziness to them. Holy crap! This reflection allowed me to own my part in my daughter's anxiety and forgive myself for my own poor decisions.

What was interesting is how I had avoided thinking about my teenage self and how she set me up for a lifetime of guilt and regret. Letting go of guilt and regret means I accept I was supposed to be on that journey in order to grow above it. Looking back at my childhood is helpful in allowing me to be a better parent and more understanding of their challenges.

I wish forgiving yourself meant you never had to experience shame, guilt, or regret again. You can make the decision that you have forgiven yourself, but the patterned thinking and emotions may still arise. Imagine being in a forest where the trees are at peace and the air is still. You can feel the serenity and love for nature because it is illustrative of how you feel inside. You have deep contentment and self-acceptance. Then *BAM*, without warning the trees start to move and you can feel the wind swirling around. You badly want it to stop and go back to the way it was, but nature is out of your hands. No matter how hard you pray or desire it, you must simply wait for it to pass. You have two choices now: sit with the discomfort of it or seek cover someplace else. This is how thoughts and emotions from the past often can disrupt our newly found peace and joy. We cannot explain why or when they will happen. You might be facing a similar situation that triggers some stored regret or fear and has brought you to remember what you did last time.

No matter where it comes from, it will throw you unless you are armed. Part of self-forgiveness is that once you do it, you don't need to do it again. God doesn't want you to beat yourself up and live with shame, guilt, or regret. You must remember these thoughts and emotions come from your Little Voice and no longer serve you. He wants you to let it go and move on with new intentions. He wants you to believe you only need to ask for forgiveness once. Although you might not believe it, I know He sent his son here to help us with forgiveness.

We know rationally we don't get do-overs. No set of circumstances will ever be the same. You can't go back in time and make different choices, even if you have worked hard to build a new identity. Life however, will often bring you second chances to demonstrate how you have changed or grown. Initially when you face one of these you might feel fearful or overwhelmed because it will seem familiar. Your Little Voice will guide you to run because it remembers how it played out in the past. It will be extremely uncomfortable for you until you become aware of what your brain is doing. It will most likely trigger your ego and start rapid firing thoughts at you. Most people don't have the power to sit back and allow all of this to pass.

The highest path through this is to acknowledge what is happening. Say to your Little Voice, "I am grateful you are trying to protect me but I no longer allow fear or anxiety to guide me. I am stronger now and can face anything with God's help." Even after you make a decision about who you really are, there may always be a battle going on inside your head. Your ego may continue to produce self-doubt and guilt, but you can remain above it.

I recently faced a situation at work that gave me a do-over moment. I bore shame and regret over how I had handled something similar in the past. After getting curious about why I felt so bad, I actually set the intention that if faced with something like it again I would take the high road. The second situation hit me out of left field. I had zero intuition it would happen, so was floored when it did. In a moment, my intentions went out the window and my Little Voice took over. I reacted and didn't respond the way I had intended. I repeated something negative about the competitor he was going to work for shocking myself as I am not someone that gossips or speaks negatively about the competition. My humanness got the absolute best of me. I also told him my opinions about what he could have done differently working for us that was totally unnecessary.

Reflecting on it later I forgave myself. I had felt betrayed and concerned about this person going to work with the competition and only wanted to warn him. His leaving fired up feelings of scarcity and not abundance. I was not detached and had expected more loyalty from him. After a few days, I acknowledged it was a mistake and apologized. It pops up sometimes even now, but I just laugh. I have zero reason to carry this guilt with me. It is over and done and I cannot do a single thing about it. The good news is that more people have quit since and I have been able to stay in my intentions and allow them to leave gracefully.

Even if you continue to make mistakes, you must remind yourself they are over and done. You can't do anything more about them. Eventually you will learn and grow from the experiences. You have already forgiven yourself so set new intentions for future similar situations and make a decision to move forward. These stored emotions will kill you if you don't learn to see them as impostors who are standing in the way of your joy.

"The weak can never forgive. Forgiveness is the attribute of the strong." Mahatma Gandhi

Balancing Our Lives

In order to have balance in your life you must put love first and start prioritizing what is really important to you. You have to be mindful and awake to do this as it takes intention every day. Usually we feel out of balance when we are not present and know in our hearts we aren't spending time where it really matters.

It still isn't exactly clear when this became such

a mainstream topic for women. I know I never heard my parent's generation talk about it. It is as if we are in a competition to do it all and as a result, we feel out of balance all the time because love loses its importance. We pour into things that don't really matter and end up without much energy at the end of the day. So many women are worn out that if we don't do something about it, chronic illnesses, addiction, mental health issues, and auto-immune disorders will continue to rise.

No matter what your schedule or priorities, you need to put family before work. I have stood by and watched many families get the devastating news that someone is terminal. Life is too short to waste it on things that don't matter as much as love. When we don't focus on what really matters, we encounter feelings of "we are not enough" because we were born to put love first. It is so easy to take your family or loved ones for granted when you are overwhelmed with life. Not prioritizing love is easier than prioritizing it. You have to approach it with discipline.

We can get better at loving others which will help us feel more balanced. I love *The Five Love Languages* by Gary Chapman and use it at home and work. We all have different needs and when we see things through someone else's eyes we can become more thoughtful and intentional. If you aren't familiar with this book, Gary introduces five love languages: personal touch, quality time, acts of service, gifts, and words of affirmation. He suggests we all have a primary and secondary love language. We tend to want and give love in the same way.

A core difference between my ex-husband and me was that we didn't have the same love languages. I constantly wanted more affection or his presence and he just gave me more gifts and did more things for me. We couldn't find a way to put one another's needs first and it slowly tore us apart. Our children demanded so much time and attention that we didn't have the energy to work on our relationship. You can have a successful marriage, even if you have different love languages. You just need to be more intentional about your relationship and give love differently to your spouse based on their love languages and not your own. We both stopped pouring into one another and lost our balance as a result of our differences.

My children and I also have different love languages. I tried to convert them both to my own because it would be easier that way, but of course I failed. I have learned to adapt how I love on them. As they grow and change their love languages may also change. Prior to the pre-teen and teenage years, my son loved affection and quality time. This made our relationship much easier because we were aligned. We connected just by watching a movie together, cuddling, or throwing a ball around. As he has grown and changed, what he needs has also shifted. He doesn't want affection now, so I just make myself available when he wants to spend time together.

My daughter has been harder to understand. It was not apparent to me what her love languages were so I tried them all. As a small child she loved affection but now it comes and goes. Over time I have realized that she wants acceptance and non-judgement preferably in the form of affirmations. We have totally different personalities so I try and pour love into her in many ways.

Males and females have different love desires. For example, men desire respect more than love where women desire love more than respect. If you disrespect a man, it becomes harder for him to ever give or receive love. Love isn't simple. You have to invest time and energy into the best way to bring it to those closest to you. I recommend that you learn more about what your needs are so you can communicate them to those around you. Then they aren't trying to guess why you feel unloved or undervalued. The most important thing we can learn is that everyone has a different way of expressing love and feeling loved. There is no right or wrong.

Before, you might have thought balance was just how you spend your time but hopefully you now can see it is a feeling that is usually tied to how present you are and how loving you are to yourself and others. I have watched people feel like they've balanced it all and have a tight schedule but then not feel fulfilled because something is missing. Balance is only achievable when you feel great about how you are showing up and you are the one that is prioritizing your life.

Putting Love First

Your old preference or desire to judge others will often come in direct conflict with love. As you sense yourself getting triggered or are overthinking, simply stop and ask yourself, "What would love say?" or "What would love do?" We often get too caught up in wanting to change others or our circumstances instead of accepting life in the moment exactly how it is.

Self-love is the most important of all loves after love for God or a higher power. The challenge with self-love for women is that no one taught us how to do this. We don't have strong role models for self-love. The women we see in the media or movies are the ones we see suffer a lot emotionally or physically. There may be a lucky few of you out there who had strong role models and easily love yourself, but most of us need to learn how. The components of self-love are acceptance, forgiveness, ability to prioritize your own needs, purpose and passion, ability to overcome negative self-talk, confidence, and a core belief you are a masterpiece. It takes work to develop strong self-love. I would start by figuring out where you are on the spectrum of each component. Then set a goal for yourself that in this year you want to gain more love for yourself and move that needle.

Think about the opposite of self-love. It is when you don't take time for yourself, don't eat healthy, don't exercise, think negative thoughts, or feel you aren't beautiful right now. If you carefully consider all the ways you don't love and nurture yourself, you can create a list of the ways you do. We often feel we need distractions from the stress or boredom in our life, but the majority of these things aren't self-love. Drinking, smoking, getting attention from men, gambling, eating, watching too much TV, gossiping, etc. all sabotage your personal goals. Although they might bring instant fun and are distracting from other stress, we tend to get down on ourselves for indulging. This vicious cycle of choosing negative thoughts or actions when we are sad or angry must stop if we are to love ourselves fully.

My soul food is simple. I practice self-love by reading, taking baths, long walks, and laughing. I take time for myself every morning and have learned how to say no. I balance my high-energy life and schedule with rest and restorative activities. Yoga is a primary practice in my life that enhances my self-love. It feeds both my body and heart. Take the time to find the unique ways you can love yourself more.

Many of us love a good romance novel. Think of your journey to love as the meeting of two lovers at the end of a good book or movie. You know your story will have a lot of ups and downs but eventually you will end up falling for yourself. If you can picture your life this way, it will help you remember your purpose.

You are born as two characters in a good romance story: the girl who doesn't love herself fully and the girl who is so loveable and is a masterpiece. At times you cherish yourself and at others you are repelled by yourself. What if your job right now is to solely pursue unconditional love and forgiveness for yourself; to love you exactly where you are right now no matter what the circumstances are or how far you have to grow? What if your job is to be accepting of your strengths and weaknesses, yet have a plan to grow and get stronger every day?

When a romance story doesn't have a happy ending it is because the two lovers cannot come together and end their conflict. The battle between them is more than the love they share. You must make a choice that your love story will have a happy ending. In spite of what happens in the world around you, loving and forgiving yourself is the only way to end self-suffering and experience true joy once and for all. Your Big Voice is your highest intelligence and it will love all parts of you. It will forgive your mistakes. It will forgive you when you hurt others or yourself. It will not hate your old self or feel guilty or shameful.

In order for the story to unfold how God intended you have to be intentional about loving yourself. I particularly like Louise Hayes' mirror work where you spend time actually saying, "I love you and accept you," in the mirror. If you have never done it, check it out on YouTube and try it for 30 days. There are too many women walking around that don't love themselves. Set time aside each day or week to be alone doing what you love. You have to really connect with what brings you joy to increase your self-love.

My romance novel is never ending. There have been times in the last 15 years that I have thought I was at the end, but found I had more work to do.

It is a journey to self-love and forgiveness, not a destination. Every day I ask, "How can I love myself even more?" True self-love contributes to higher confidence and energy that you can use to spread more joy and love. Anything external can be taken away from us, including those who love us. We must love and enjoy ourselves so that when people or things are lost, we can still be joyful.

Learning to love you and have self-compassion needs to be a daily practice. It seems ridiculous to not be born that way or maybe we were and our upbringing or society stole it from us. When you want so badly to be joyful, faithful, and purpose-ful, yet find yourself in a season where you are irritable, critical or have self-pity you must remain accepting and non-judgmental of yourself. No matter the reason or stress that has caused it, remain aware you are likely projecting this neg-ativity. We are human and have formed in our brains years of deep pathways that lead to negativity. Although you want to form a new pathway that overrides your struggle or uncer-tainty, it won't happen overnight.

We can get overwhelmed and have nothing to give. Whether it is our physical health or emo-tional health, if we aren't cautiously taking care of our own needs we will eventually burn out. I have worked for years on spiritual and personal growth and know that nothing makes you immune to this. You might even come to believe you can handle anything with grace, but then *BAM* something happens. The best way to show yourself love is through self-care.

As I write this, I am in a place where I must increase my self-love and compassion. My sister is still in jail and her future is uncertain. I am surrendered to the uncertainty that my life has, yet my Little Voice is battling me to take action and challenge things daily. I am physically and emotionally fatigued. I have no idea if I need rest and alone time or I need fun and support with people I love. I am for the first time in my life allowing myself to be fully sad and not distracted. I remain committed to not taking any of this out on others. I still practice my disciplines and show up for others, but inside my heart is shattered.

Having more self-love and compassion means that I must put myself first. It is an important part of my healing journey because before I would have always jumped to my sister's rescue. I am sad that her life and the lives of her children are forever changed but in order to put myself first I will let go of saving her, making decisions for her, or worrying about her. Loving me means trusting God more.

Choosing Love over Significance

Which one will you choose? You cannot have both simultaneously. It is possible, however, that you may be choosing one in one area of your life and one in another. Love is the highest priority of your Big Voice and significance is the highest priority of your Little Voice.

Love is about giving, not receiving. It is about being intentional and kind and managing our triggers so we don't hurt others. Love is being on the journey. Love is about putting our fears aside and jumping headfirst into the unknown all while being present in each moment. Love is being compassionate to our differences and serving others who need us. It is humble and passionate. It is peace and fulfillment with complete detachment.

Significance is the opposite. It is about getting not giving. It is about maintaining your human will, not God's. It's about feeding your Little Voice's need for attention. Significance is about accumulating money, awards, or material things so we feel good about ourselves. Significance says I am better or more important than others. It is an endless pit of human desire that lacks any inner peace or contentment. It is attached to outcomes and will destroy others when trying to gain what it wants. Significance believes it matters how others see you rather than how you make others feel. It is manipulative; craving affirmation and recognition.

It is easy to be tricked by significance. You have to take a close look at your life and relationships to understand how you are prioritizing how other people see you over how you are feeling. Before, to anyone looking in from the outside, I appeared to be an emotionally intelligent, grateful, and kind woman. On the inside though I was obsessed with changing everything about myself I had identified as "wrong." Quite literally I was striving to be perfect even after I believed I had beaten that desire. Significance had tricked me into thinking self-improvement was the same as self-love. Once I realized I was prioritizing rescuing others over my own emotional and physical well-being, I quickly reset my priorities.

Toward the end of my mother's life, as I sat by her bed for days on end in stillness, it finally sunk in that nothing except love matters. She could only say my name and the word love during her last three months. She tried so hard to say all three precious words "I love you" but couldn't string them together. I believe she was a human sacrifice on my journey to finally let me see I had still been prioritizing significance over love.

Since then I can see significance show up in my life so clearly. My Little Voice never fails to create cravings but my Big Voice has the power to override them. I no longer beat myself up when the thoughts arise that are not in alignment with who I really am. I stop and ask myself, why am I doing this? Am I doing it out of love, or has the enemy or my Little Voice become sneakier? It is amazing how much social media triggers this for all of us . . . as if the number of likes or views really matter. Because I have become aware, the second I sense significance creeping in I can easily self-correct.

My job and purpose create situations where I get a large share of attention and recognition. My intention is to remain humbly confident and give God the glory. I firmly believe He created us to be all love. Any time something falls outside of love, I know I need to be armed to fight it.

You can start choosing love today by watching what love and significance say or think, and then giving yourself space to respond rather than react. Doing so will grow your level of joy when you realize how powerful you are to change your life.

Walking through Pain and Shame
We all carry the past with us. Sometimes we know

it and other times we don't. Some wounds of the past are deeper than others but the common denominator is they steal your joy and appear in daily decisions, thoughts, and emotions without you asking them to.

You can have varying degrees of pain or shame that rule your daily life and habits. Your ego or Little Voice draws from them to make decisions that protect you from more pain. Shame feeds self-doubt and pity, and steals your confidence. Escaping pain and shame is the only way to heal whether you created it, someone else did, or you have lost loved ones. You can never remove the pain or shame; you can only transcend it and become more powerful because of it. You don't get to choose the story of your life, nor do you get to go back and have a do-over, but you can find lessons in it all. Choosing to deal with pain and shame on a conscious level will ensure you aren't triggered as often subconsciously.

Understanding the past and the effects pain and shame had on you, can help you relate and feel compassion for others who have experienced similar situations. For example, if a woman comes across hardened and closed-hearted, it might be attached to the fear of loss she endured in her past . . . she simply doesn't want to be open to getting hurt again. The pain or shame is causing her to stop being open-hearted in fear the same thing will happen again. Rather than judge her you give her more love and encouragement in anticipation of her walls eventually coming down.

Pain and suffering are different. Pain is the event or wound and suffering is the constant thinking or focus on the pain. As women we hypothesize a lot and tend to get into our heads over pain easily. The ability to quickly move on after we deal with our pain is not something we were taught very well. We may have been shamed for hurting and heard "big girls don't cry" and never fully learned how to process pain.

I hear over and over again women describe themselves as strong. Yet most of these women just pretend their pain and shame don't exist and they go through life being a caretaker; emptying themselves into others, never taking care of their own needs. Not dealing with pain and shame is not being strong and eventually you will suffer. You have to walk through the pain or shame to find your true power.

Pain can be deep in your subconscious mind and appear as an emotional response. It generally produces fear that turns into sadness, anxiety, or anger. It will continuously pop up in your life and guide your decisions until you walk through it. Similar to forgiveness, it is a process that will free you of any stored emotional baggage.

Most of us have experienced painful events in our lifetime. They vary in degree based on the duration and severity. Whether you are a victim of abuse, were abandoned, lost a loved one, or hurt yourself or others, most of us have experienced some pretty severe things. The loss of love from someone who is significant can also trigger intense pain. We may feel pain when our self-esteem or confidence has been shaken.

If you are a believer, it is important you accept that God didn't create the pain for you to suffer. He doesn't call people to pain to allow you to grow stronger. Life happens and we cannot avoid tragedies or abuse. Disease occurs and people die. It may come from environmental or health choices or be completely random. He doesn't lead people to abuse you or abandon you. He is there to help you through whatever you need Him to help you with. He is the one that will never abandon or judge you. You cannot ask *where* He was when the pain happened. You cannot ask why it happened. These questions cannot be answered on earth and will only stop your healing process. The mysteries of this place cannot be revealed while you are here. It is up to us to accept we cannot understand everything.

So how do you walk through pain and shame?

You first have to make a commitment of time. You can enter this process alone or with a therapist or life coach. You have to admit that you have not yet fully faced the depth of pain, acceptance, and forgiveness necessary to heal. I would recommend blocking a few hours that you can dedicate to this. Grab a journal or notebook and write down the event or season around which you have pain or shame. Then write down the emotions associated with it. In the next section write down all the triggers that bring out this pain or emotional response. I include the names of the people who are associated with it as well. I then recommend recognizing the value, preference, or standard that the pain is in opposition to. For example:

Pain/Shame: Ending my marriage

Emotions: Blame, Anger, Resentment, Failure

I blame myself for staying too long. I blame my ex for being passive and not more driven. I am angry he didn't fight for us. I am sad our children live in separate homes. I am resentful he couldn't change and is not physically healthy.

Triggers:

- New relationship anxiety where I sense the same thing may happen again and I will fail
- When our kids have his tendencies or are withdrawn
- When I get tired and overwhelmed I wish I

had a provider to take care of things

- When two households cause me extra work
- Lack of control with kids

People affected: My ex, me, kids, and men I date

Preferences/Standards/Values not met:

- I would prefer he was stronger and more dominant
- I would prefer I was more patient, loving and kind
- I would prefer I was more accepting and non-judgmental of our differences
- I would prefer he was goal-oriented and growth-minded
- I would prefer he was more passionate, healthy, and driven

The next step is to find gratitude in the pain and shame. These are the lessons or good things that may have come from it. If you have had a painful life, this may require more effort for you to find.

Gratitude:

- Two beautiful kids
- Co-parenting partner who is kind and dependable
- Amazing ex-husband who would be there for me no matter what
- Personal growth and acceptance that I

made my share of mistakes and it was my mindset that created much of my self-suffering

- Acceptance I was not compatible with him from the beginning but didn't yet know my authentic self

Once you find gratitude the next step is to forgive everyone involved. As you will learn, forgiveness doesn't require letting a person back into your life, but rather just accepting their brokenness. Forgiveness requires acknowledging those things you feel responsible for and letting go of any shame. Forgiveness removes the desire to blame and replaces it with an acceptance that most people do the best they can with the life path they have been given. You may have anger and pain from an abuser that makes it extremely difficult to find gratitude. You aren't finding gratitude for what happened or for them per se but you have to find gratitude in what you have become in spite of what happened. Many abusers were victims of abuse or were in proximity to others who didn't elevate their thinking or behavior. It is impossible to know why they did what they did so letting go of finding the why will lead you to letting go faster.

Forgiveness:
- Myself for choosing someone I wanted to

change; for lacking acceptance, being judgmental, not knowing what he needed; not identifying wanting an equal partner who was growth-minded and driven

- My ex for not fighting for us and being honest with me about how I made him feel

After you have forgiven yourself and anyone else involved, you need a plan to handle this pain and shame when something in life triggers it. Your plan should include quieting your ego so you can remain open-hearted. You don't want fear to run your life, but you can set healthy boundaries or standards. For example, if a past relationship was painful because your ex drank too much, setting a standard that you won't date someone who abuses alcohol is a great decision.

Plan:
- Identifying when I am triggered
- Identifying when this pain shows up in my relationship
- Be accepting and non-judgmental
- Be clear on standards for new relationships
- Accept my ex for who he is and be grateful for him

There is no way to escape feelings that might pop up, but you can make a decision they won't disrupt your life vision. Sitting with sadness or pain for a bit won't disrupt your life, but obsessing or hypothesizing will. Remember to use your TMS when you feel yourself becoming obsessive about your past. Bringing the pain and shame out of the darkness is essential to your healing.

Parenting

The opportunity to parent my amazing kids has been my greatest teacher in remaining mindful. They keep me centered on this path. I was raised by parents who provided for us the best they could. Like most families there was not a lot of intentional parenting because everyone was just trying to make ends meet. They weren't mean or pessimistic but we didn't have deep conversations about mindset or values.

My dad wanted us to be financially successful and look presentable. My mom had a short list as well – she wanted us to be independent, important, and thin. They both wanted more for us than they had for themselves. My mom placed a high value on physical appearance. She carefully watched her weight, sometimes only drinking coffee and eating baby carrots. I am honestly surprised she didn't turn orange! Watching the new show "This is Us" I saw my mom in Rebecca, the mother who is overly concerned with her daughter's weight. This impacted both my sister and I negatively. What I didn't expect as I watched that show was to see myself as the mother, too. I had swung the pendulum so far that I created too much pressure for my daughter to not repeat the mistakes I made. I became too intentional. It is difficult to find that happy medium.

Because I had done a great deal of work on understanding my own childhood, I was able to create a parenting vision that was a combo of things I liked that my parents did, things I didn't like, and things I read or heard. I listed the top values I wanted for my children and set my intentions. My awareness allowed me to respond to triggers and not be reactive. I read books and took courses on parenting. It is amazing to me how so many parents stop after reading *What to Expect When You are Expecting* and then switch to autopilot.

My children are well-behaved and loving, but man, can they trigger some strong preferences. My desire is they are loving and kind, responsible, trying their hardest when appropriate, and are disciplined. Then add on that I want them emotionally open and able to communicate with me when they need help. Needless to say, based on my preferences, there are a lot of opportunities for me to be triggered. Keep in mind I am not looking for my kids to be perfect but having a vision keeps me focused on what I am trying to develop not what I expect of them. My awareness opens space to not react and to respond appropriately instead of attacking them when they aren't following the rules or they trigger a preference. My intention is to always remain calm and not lose my temper.

Unfortunately, if I am exhausted and have limited energy this becomes almost impossible to do. My "go to" is to dump everything on them that they need to be doing differently not just address the current issue. I end up talking AT my kids instead of trying to teach or guide them. I can minimize this by setting up a more predictable plan. For example, my son uses timers, which cut down on both our frustrations. When he knows exactly what to plan for, transitioning from one thing to another is easier. His most common response had been, "One more minute, Mom," which used to drive me crazy.

Remember you have two options with triggers: grow through them or make a plan to avoid them. If you are a parent you know it is really hard to avoid having our kids fire us up so choosing to grow is really our best option. Create plans around specific things that piss you off regularly. Our kids are much more predictable once we start documenting their behaviors. There is a down-loadable Trigger Management Plan on the Big

Voices website where you can create a plan for reoccurring triggers.

Here are some examples of what I have done: If you love being on time and your kids are always running late, you probably need a combo of growth and avoidance. Setting schedules up beforehand that leave a little extra time will help. Let go of the idea that schedules are always hard and fast and realize sometimes they can be more relaxed. If it is to a flight or event with a cutoff, those are not negotiable, but there are other things we can be attached to that really don't matter like the high school football game or a friend's birthday party. Even if they don't say it, our kids crave more freedom and flexibility in their over-scheduled lives.

After I read an amazing letter to parents from a mom who lost her son to a heroin overdose I changed my perspective on many things that had been triggering me around responsibility. I was getting frustrated with missed assignments and forgotten backpacks, but was enabling my kids by always rescuing them. The mom's story was that she too did this and regretted it. She will never fully understand the reason for her son's suffering or addiction, but when she sent him to college he had a hard time coping on his own. He was so used to having his mom help him that he turned to drugs originally just to stay focused.

Learning to be super-clear with our kids and having intentions set before we get into situations is the best approach. Our responsibility is to send them into the world one day to be contributing members of society, yet we think they were born knowing what to do. Most parents' default is their own experience. For a few this might work, but for the rest of us we need skills and mentorship. We need a plan and awareness to help us improve.

Not everyone had a positive upbringing that led them to become a loving adult. Some people endured emotional, physical, or sexual abuse the rest of us could never imagine. Choosing to bring children into this world is a huge responsibility where trust and forgiveness are required daily. If you don't have children yet, but are planning to at some point, I highly advise working through self-love, forgiveness, and trust before you do.

Monthly Cycles

There are cycles in a month when as women we might encounter major emotional disturbances. Sometimes this dramatic change in mood cannot be explained by anything externally. It can happen so quickly . . . one minute we are filled with joy, and the next minute we slip into suffering and our thoughts are spinning out of control. Our hormones need to be in a delicate balance for us to feel at our best.

Most women can pinpoint a major shift as their hormones change and they realize their period is coming. Someone you looked at adoringly yesterday becomes disgusting or irritating to you today without them doing a single thing differently. You might have been able to stick to your TMS yesterday but now your PMS has taken over. Today you know you are under attack and feel powerless in quieting your mind. You may be completely committed to maintaining your Big Voice, but then *BAM* you know your hormones are out of balance and there is nothing that you can do about it. I believe God gave this to women because He knew we were the superior sex. He evened things out a bit to give men a fair chance against us.

I become extremely uncomfortable during this time and focus more on pain or shame. I want to focus on my suffering. I feel sorry for myself and all that I carry. The same thoughts repeat themselves monthly and are as predictable as the sun rising and setting. Most women I know also experience these monthly shifts. If you're one of the rare few who don't, be extremely grateful!

Hormonal changes are easy to blame for our

emotional changes yet we just need to be aware of them so they have less power over our lives. We can rise above and not react to their guidance. We can be more mindful and respond to anything that triggers us rather than react and be hurtful. I recommend that rather than seeing your monthly cycle as a bad thing, you find gratitude in this season. Recognizing you are an emotional, unique creature will help you remain content. I now laugh at my hormones when they show up. I use humor to see my emotions they create rather than self-pity.

I view my emotional ups and downs separate from my authentic self. Knowing I am healthy spiritually and that any disturbance will pass allows me to remain consistent in how I live my life. I understand how my emotions and thinking change in a 30-day timeframe so that I can prepare and be ready for it. I am simply a watcher of the thoughts and emotions and choose to not react.

My gut reaction when the cycle starts is to question, "What is wrong with me?" That is a cue that I am under attack because my highest self would never ask such a ridiculous question. It knows there is nothing wrong with my imperfect self! I have written a letter to myself that I read only when I am going through this monthly struggle. In it, I give myself instructions on how to handle things and hope that it will pass quickly. The bad days, and my awareness of them, have led me to be more grateful for the other 28 days. If actually documented it, we would probably see more women end relationships or quit their jobs during this time simply because we are so sensitive.

I am so grateful I am a woman who can experience the benefits of our hormonal system. Our ability to nurture, connect, and relate to others is generally higher than that of males. The hormones that change during pregnancy and after childbirth are an amazing illustration of how masterful the life cycle is. We have bonding hormones that ensure we will take care of our babies. Whether you have children or not, you have benefited from them; some of your spark and desire in life comes from them.

When we age our hormones shift again. This hormonal fluctuation may cause more changes as we enter the pre-menopausal, menopausal, and post-menopausal years. Estrogen decreases and testosterone increases. This may explain why more women awaken in their early 50's. They might be done taking care of everyone else and finally rise up to become their highest self. Parenting no longer comes with the same responsibilities and time for them may be more abundant. If you look around at church meetings, charity events, or in political settings to name a few, you will see more women who are older than younger. Maybe they have more capacity or maybe their hormones have shifted in such a way they can no longer sit back and not do anything about the injustices in the world.

A goal of the Big Voices movement is to wake up women earlier. Better yet, let's start with not letting our young girls follow in our footsteps. Let's keep them awake. The world would benefit from an army of women committed to authenticity and contribution. In order for this to happen, you need to better understand your body and how it changes. I would recommend you add this to your growth plan so you are more educated on how your body and hormones work. *The Female Brain* by Dr. Louann Brizendine does an excellent job of explaining it.

Our hormones can cause negative feelings but only if we let them. They can make us needy and crave things that are not good for us. As you track your cycle, be sure to watch how your thoughts and emotions change so you can be more intentional about not letting them sabotage your vision or goals. You can live more consistently in spite of the disturbances they cause.

Battling Loneliness

As I shared earlier, one way we can suffer is through loneliness. The distance between me and the rest of the world seems to be increasing lately so it has shown up more. As I become more awake to the biases and preferences our egos produce I am less allured by them. I cannot get caught up in meaningless conversations or pleasure-seeking activities like I used to. I am without a desire to fit in or be significant any longer. It has in some ways become lonely. It may become lonely for you too until you are comfortable with the new story you are writing and find more like-minded people to connect with.

I used to love partying and losing myself in the alcohol I drank. A day at the pool bar followed by a night dancing into the late hours was my idea of a great vacation. It was so easy to connect with others and feel like a part of something. Drinks clanking, dirty-dancing, and mega-fun were what I needed to classify a night as amazing. The discontentment I felt was momentarily quieted when I became too intoxicated to remember. I never hurt anyone else, but I did hurt myself as good choices were traded for what felt good in the moment. The day after a "good" night was usually filled with physical exhaustion and/or sickness mixed with laughter with friends as we rehashed the night's happenings.

Fast forward years into my awakening – I am on a business awards trip sitting on a balcony in Cabo looking at a beautiful view. I spent four days and three nights entertaining our top sales team. While they are having fun they have no idea of the inner turmoil I am facing. Loneliness arises as it is tough for me to connect with others on this trip when they are hammered and I am not. Guilt and shame arises as I recount too many late Cabo nights of the past. Memories of previous all-star trips over a 15 year period come flooding back. My ex and I always fought at them. I am sure it is because he didn't conform to my preferences and I punished him for his behavior. I know now when you place high expectations on others you will always be disappointed. There was the time he upgraded to first class and was hammered by the time he arrived at the hotel. (We flew separate throughout our marriage). Or the time he got a life-threatening coral cut, which pretty much ended our fun.

These trips always caused a level of disruption for me. I was never comfortable because I was always chasing the wind and setting myself up for disappointment as my expectations were too high. Now single, the last four years I have brought along two friends and two boyfriends to these events. All of them still drink so they easily fit in with everyone else. It has left me feeling like an outsider peering into a party from a window. There are moments I wish I could let go and join them again and other moments I have zero desire to participate.

The challenge in walking this loneliness line comes with finding peace and acceptance in the conflict that exists between the person you were and the person you are becoming. Personal growth during this season of your life doesn't mean you judge others. You have to determine if you can grow through your differences with them or you need to avoid them. Above all, you have to maintain your authenticity. The people who are on the Booze Cruise of life (thank you, Christiane Northrup, for that metaphor) all believe you aren't fun or have something wrong with you when you don't participate. They will persuade you to join them or quietly judge you as "boring."

This valley between the worlds you exist in can be extremely uncomfortable. There are people who will understand that you find more joy in solitude or relaxing than drinking or partying. But they are out there. You cannot fall into self-pity or loneliness on this journey. Fortunately, there are many purpose-driven women committed to growth to discover and if we change our perspective we can find renewed connection with people that have always been in our lives.

You can still enjoy all the friendships you had, but how you enjoy them might change a little. Maybe instead of meeting at your usual bar, you take a walk or get coffee. Identify upfront what situations trigger your judgment or self-pity and strive to avoid them. Over time you might grow through them and become more accepting, but in the beginning avoidance may be key as you don't want to become derailed. Just like an alcoholic should avoid a bar until they are certain they are strong enough, you must avoid situations that make you feel like something is wrong with you.

Letting go of your false self is the most freeing thing you can do. Just expect a little loneliness and know that it will pass.

Being Meek

Meek is a word you most likely believe to be a bad thing. You have been taught that the strong and fittest survive and thrive. You watch pushy people force themselves into better positions and weaker people get stepped on. Whether within a social circle, a company, or a family, you have been shown it is better to stand up aggressively for what you believe.

Meek doesn't mean weak. It means being powerful without taking action. It is a strategy you must maintain to achieve the highest level of spiritual success. Meekness is important is because not everyone is ready for our power and strength. Sometimes we have to hold back to make the biggest impact. For women trying to get ahead in business, this may seem counterintuitive. We have watched women enter a man's world and become forced to abandon our values and femininity to get ahead. We have become masculine to prove our worth. We have abandoned balance, joy, and peace to gain more prosperity or respect. For our families, we try to transition quickly to being a nurturer once at home. This effort usually falls short and we end up running our homes like a business forgetting to prioritize love and laughter. Even for women who don't work outside the home or don't have families it is a struggle to know when to use our power. We often confuse it with control which eventually backfires.

There is a way to stay in our natural essence, whether feminine or masculine, and use our power differently to massively impact the world. We have to learn to become more strategic about how we live. We cannot always get what we want by being controlling or dominating. We need to learn how to be meek at times. This requires a vision and plan. It requires discipline and self-awareness. You will need to temper your urge to do something right now. It requires massive patience and a belief that life happens for you.

The world is dependent on us learning to be meek. Too many people view women trying to make a change as irrational or ill-equipped to run big companies or our nation. In order to rise up together and unite against all of the injustice, we need to grow together and support one another. We have to better understand interpersonal relationships so we know when and when not, to use our power. Meek isn't being passive. It isn't that you aren't ever speaking up or taking action, you are just waiting for the right time. There are many situations where being meek will help you suffer less. So much conflict in our life is because we use our power too soon and it backfires.

"A strong woman looks a challenge in the eye and gives it a wink." Gina Carey

For example, your boss just made a major decision with which you disagree. He runs the company, so he is entitled to do whatever he wants regardless of your opinion. You are blown away by his decision and believe it will negatively impact both the culture and success of the organization. You want badly to tell him this and to try and change his mind. Your awareness will tell you this is pointless. You should choose to be meek. Vet out his new decision, accepting it will unfold exactly how it is supposed to even if that means it doesn't work. You should not complain about it to others or try to make his decision fail because negative thoughts and actions will only impact you negatively and keep you from your truth. Be open to the endless possibilities his decision has created. You cannot get attached to your belief that it is a bad decision. It is simply not a decision you would have made. You must remain supportive and trust if his decision is wrong it will reveal itself over time on its own. We often bring our own drama by trying to sabotage something we don't agree with making us look bad in the end. Although it might feel good to complain about your boss in the short-term, it is not getting you closer to increased joy or reduced suffering.

As humans if we ever feel 100 percent right about something it should be an early indicator our Little Voice or ego has been fired up and is ready to lead us down the wrong path. Whether what you felt sure about succeeds or fails doesn't matter. Life is not black and white and there are a million ways things can turn out. In the prior example, it is something to be celebrated if you refrained from giving your opinion and remained supportive even when you disagreed. Your career may actually improve when you are meek and more patient in how you handle things.

When we try to use our power solely to get what we want we are often seen as controlling bitches. As unfair as it is, we aren't viewed the same as a powerful man who might be praised for the same behavior. We have to accept this gender bias to ultimately gain ground within our homes, businesses, and in politics. If we use our power more effectively, if we practice being meek and patient, we will have more opportunity.

Being of Service

Beyond finding more joy and reducing your suffering comes a much higher purpose. The world needs you to discard your self-absorption and make a massive impact in the lives of others. Most of us can get trapped in our own little worlds worrying about insignificant things. We need to serve more and fight for the children or people that may never have a chance without us. Serving and supporting others will raise the joy and gratitude you feel and help you experience more connection.

In the U.S. and the world, millions of children

are born into poverty or abusive homes. Their parents were probably born into similar situations and didn't know how to rise above them. Without access to education or a safe environment it is unlikely that these children will be able to break the cycle. Whether the child will turn to illegal activity or addiction or become a respectable member of society is unknown. All humans want to be a part of something and feel connected. Many of these children will become a part of the tribe (or gangs) who surrounded them. We must find more ways to mentor and guide them.

There are few exceptions, but on rare occasions you will hear the story of a child who goes on to Harvard and changes the world. We don't hear the stories of all the children left behind. We eventually see the devastation that poverty causes through news stories. It can be incredibly difficult for these children to choose a different life.

I recently had dinner with some teenagers at a state-run home in Florida. They had a mix of personalities, some outgoing and cheery, some dark and depressed. My heart hurt knowing there was only a slim chance they would become law-abiding adults. I could sense the separation between us and the feeling of abandonment in the room. Although my group was there to support them and give them a break from their usual routine – it was only one night.

I spent most of my time with two girls. I was drawn to one girl in particular. I felt instantly if she had been born into a higher socioeconomic environment with a supportive family she could be anything she wanted. She had natural strength and appeared super-confident. Behind this though I could see her heart had hardened. She was 16 and had been in the home for over two years. I could see pain and abandonment in her eyes that would take years to work through if she ever had the opportunity. I see our Big Voices as a way to give this opportunity to her and so many others.

There are a million ways for you to serve and get involved. You just need to make it a goal and get disciplined about it. Start small and make an effort, your Big Voice will thank you because of all the goodness it will bring to you personally and the impact it will have on the world.

Meditation

Meditating is a proven activity that will help bring you more peace, clarity, and will strengthen your immune system. Many women believe they can't do it, especially type-A women like me. It is humorous when we try and quiet our minds, sit still, and be without thought. It may seem unimaginable to dedicate time to yourself each day and empty your mind but I promise if you try, you will love the effect it has on your life. It takes dedication and failure to figure out what works for you.

There are many different types of meditation that range from spiritual to focused attention. The common denominator amongst the hundreds or thousands of types is that they involve breathing and effortless presence. I can assure you at first no matter what type you try, your Little Voice will kick and scream when you meditate because your Little Voice does not want you to see how separate it is from your authentic self.

New studies show that meditation is proven to increase our healing power. One study, found in the journal *Circulation: Cardiovascular Quality and Outcomes*, shows those that took a transcendental meditation class reduced their overall risk of heart disease 48%. Other studies have shown that the brains of those who meditate show higher levels of gyrification (folding of the cerebral cortex). This can help us process information better. (*Frontiers in Human Neuroscience Feb 2012.*)

When learning to meditate, it may be helpful to remove yourself from daily life and go somewhere where masters can teach you. I love the Chopra Center in Carlsbad as a great center to learn to meditate more effectively. If traveling to a center isn't possible, you can still watch tons of videos on YouTube. There is no right or wrong approach to learning. Yoga and meditation will help you become more present if you give them a chance. Even if you are distracted and can't let go, these practices will still be of benefit to you.

I was fortunate to meet Elizabeth Gilbert at a Women's Conference in Long Beach shortly after her book, *Eat, Pray, Love* had been published. She helped me to understand I was not alone in this journey to meditate correctly. She shared a story of when she was in India in a meditation her mind wandered to where she should go in a year. She thought about making a meditation room, what colors to make it and how she would afford it. She quickly caught herself and realized that although she was in one of the most sacred places to meditate she too was also powerless to her mind trying to take over. She made me remember there is no wrong or right and all we should celebrate is our intention to be present.

In addition to daily meditation techniques, there are purposeful meditations you can do as well. These may include guided techniques that are designed to go back in time and heal things you may have blocked. I did a guided meditation at a Hay House event in Las Vegas recently that changed my life. Dr. Christiane Northrup is an amazing and wise OBGYN who promotes spirituality and healing as a way to prevent disease. I had no idea when she started this journey what would happen. She guided us back to find our self between the ages of five and ten. I immediately chose the age of seven. As I drifted back I didn't expect to meet myself there. But, as tears flowed down my face . . . I found a stressed out seven-year-old waiting for me in a field of beautiful flowers. I could feel she was already concerned she wasn't smart enough or important enough. I knew going into this meditation that my Little Voice or ego started to take over at a young age, but I had no idea I would meet the girl who was already less joyful or playful because she was so worried about what everyone else was thinking. It was hard seeing her so sad. As we walked together, she asked "why don't you love me?" I realized in that moment, that I had stopped loving her and my former self because I didn't love all the decisions or choices they made. I had judged her and felt sorry for her. I held her close and let her know we were no longer trapped and it was time to fully let go. Although I had been meditating on and off over the years, the emotional surge I experienced during this exercise was the most intense I had had in years. It made me see I hadn't prioritized fun from a young age and had put way too much pressure on myself which I carried into adulthood.

Part of the pain of the perfectionist is not being able to be present and free to release whatever you are feeling. It paralyzes your ability to be as emotional as everyone else. I realize now I created internal conflict that divided me. I had pushed my former self aside instead of loving her and forgiving her. All she needed was my assurance that she was loved and valued. I don't know why she sought it externally so much, but I shared everything I now know with her. She relaxed in my embrace and said, "I love you." My unconditional love and acceptance was what that little girl needed but when I awakened, for many years, I chose to hate and resent her. I created my own conflict and suffering without even realizing it. If anyone asked me if I loved myself completely I would have answered yes without realizing this was not the truth. I was embarrassed and carried shame for all the choices I had made before but in that meditation I finally let go and accepted it was a necessary part of my life.

On this journey, you will always keep learning. There is no final destination or ending to it. You have to remain open-hearted and growth-minded to fully embrace all the wisdom and knowledge that exists. Even though I had done work for years I was still open going into that guided meditation and had an aha moment that changed my life forever.

My goals and purpose aren't set in stone. I am still open to going wherever God guides me. After realizing that I needed to love all of myself including my old self, I went back and added "I Am" statements to my daily list as reminders. I added I AM vibrant and playful. I added stop the self-pity and loneliness to my goals. I also added make more like-minded friends. I hadn't realized that I was punishing myself for who I was. I had stopped being that adventurous and free child at the early age of seven and needed to start prioritizing fun again.

You can always keep growing your authentic self. That is why you must remain open-hearted and never believe you have arrived at your final destination. Meditation can help fuel your curiosity and creativity. When I give my brain rest from all its thinking, I return more clear and centered. It helps me release tension or stored energy from any triggers I may have encountered throughout the day.

Although having your own *Eat, Pray, Love* trip would be amazing so you could dedicate a massive amount of time to meditating, all you need is a few minutes a day. Just stop and breathe whenever you can wherever you are. I practice stoplight meditations daily where instead of being like the hundreds of other people that check their phones I simply mediate on things I am grateful for.

Laughter

It is no secret, as you look around, that most of us have heaviness about us. Not the kind that comes from eating a large pepperoni pizza, but the kind that feels like we have the weight of the world on our shoulders. You can see it as impatience which sets in when there's a long line at Starbucks or in traffic when someone in a rush cuts numerous people off just to get ahead of a few cars. You can see it on the sports field as parents yell at their kids or pace back and forth. You can see it at work when budgets are off or markets are down. There is so much stress and so little lightheartedness.

We know stress is not good for us. Stress releases cortisol, a natural enemy for our physical body. We cannot sleep, we start projecting, and we lose hope when we are feeling overwhelmed or heavy with life's burdens. So what helps besides getting clear on your priorities, living more mindfully, and being aware that most of what we carry or worry about is nonsense? Laughter! Nothing feeds our souls and has the power to offset pain more than a good belly laugh.

If you are feeling like life is too much right now, you probably think you have nothing to laugh about or no one in your life is funny. Don't worry. I am going to give you a plan to pull yourself out of it. First, remember back to when you were a kid without all the heaviness on your shoulders. Your only mission on a summer night was to be home by dark and make it for dinner. You were adventurous and light. You spent time with friends giggling over just about anything – maybe it was the clerk at the drug store with blue hair or the two boys that walked by with Playboys hidden. You noticed things . . . you laughed . . . you had fun. It was your biggest priority!

Now, because you have so much on your plate you're likely to spend more time complaining than laughing. You can change by being more intentional. With the internet and Netflix it is easier than ever to find things that make us laugh. So where do you start? There are two areas you can change that will cultivate more lightness and laughter.

The first part is rather than beat yourself up for any mistake or humanness you have you are trying to grow through, replace it with laughter.

Simply shift your words and thoughts from "I can't believe I just did that. What is wrong with me?" to "Holy crap! That was hilarious! I just lost it. I wish I had it on video." On this journey we are not shooting for perfection, only progress so your willingness to see your struggles as funny rather than stupid will drastically change how you feel.

As you look at your life use a lens that frames things differently. Start looking for things that are funny rather than just sitting with frustration. You can do this in two ways: through your own experiences and by priming the pump. So either look for humor in your own life or bring more humor in through movies, videos, or seeing a comedian.

Starting with your own life, simply make a shift. You set your intentions before your day starts by committing to laughing at yourself more. I recently had a great opportunity to do this. I received an email from one of the managers who works for me with some information about a transaction. I opened it while on a conference call that was wasting my time. Rather than take the time to read any of his prior emails, I fired back questions for him. My perception was that he wanted me to make the decision for him so my emails came across that I was annoyed. We went back and forth about five times before he poked his head into my door. I was still on the call so waved him off, but before he left he just said, "My earlier email asked you to approve it so I'm just wondering why you are questioning me." I sat there for a moment before I opened the earlier email and just laughed. He probably thought I didn't trust him. In my email I had said, "I will not make decisions for you . . . you need to manage this aspect of your business" when in fact he had already made the decision, but I missed it.

A few lessons here for me. First, I am committed to not multitasking and this reminds me why. Second, I should start at the oldest email because so much communication is sequential and I could miss something. Third, I am human and will still get triggered so it is best to view making mistakes as reminders that life is funny. I apologized publicly to him as I shared this story in a group coaching session because rather than pretending managing triggers is easy, I have learned to be open about them.

The second part is framing your life differently. If you compare people's lives to a movie genre, most would be a drama or suspense thriller and a few might even say their life is a horror film. Your job is to shift and call your life a comedy. Recognizing you are the director of your life, you must start capturing more funny scenes. And if you don't have enough, you must create them – seek out movies, events, or people that fill you with laughter. The only way for life to be lighter is to look at it differently. You have a choice.

Laughter is truly the best medicine and will improve your physical well-being as well as your mental health. If you feel your life is too serious, make an effort to work on it. Add laughter and fun to your vision. I can assure you, your relationships will change as well. You can be successful and fun at the same time.

A COUNTINUING JOURNEY

"What will matter is the good we did, not the good we expected others to do." Elizabeth Lesser

There many people who wake up but eventually either fall back into their old way of living or complain they wish it wasn't so hard. Living mindfully will continuously take your energy and commitment. You cannot expect your life to get easier. It is only how you get through things that will be easier. You can easily overestimate awareness as freedom from suffering when in actuality becoming mindful is a daily practice and journey. You must learn to celebrate small victories and steps and not expect your entire life to change overnight.

You may encounter questions along the way like "why is my life not getting easier?" or "why am I still having problems?" This is your Little Voice trying to lure you back into self-pity or self-loathing. You need to stay strong and remember the purpose of finding your Big Voice. You can cultivate joy and reduce suffering if you stay centered on your new mindset. It may take years to fully step into your newfound awareness with nothing but gratitude and love.

Awareness is achieved by making a decision that you are not your thoughts and they will no longer control or run your life. To be effective you must be hormonally balanced and emotionally capable. It is important to see your physician and ensure that nothing medically is working against you. If you suffer from mental illness, you may not have the ability to always stay in your Big Voice but you can still practice all the strategies you find here. All you are looking for is space; a gap between a thought or emotion and your response so you may see it for what it is. Once you have this you will be able to practice Thought Management Strategy (TMS).

It may take days, weeks, or months to sift through your triggers or preferences. The longer you practice mindfulness though the faster it will become. I have had to dedicate some serious time and energy in the past to get through some of my faulty programming. Just remember managing your triggers can be super-fun and rewarding as you start responding and not reacting. You can break past cycles and keep from beating yourself up for how you handled something.

Time goes by so fast. The world needs you to be strong and loud. Do not waste another moment living in self-suffering or without joy. Quit being taken advantage of because you are on autopilot. Too many other women need you to find your power and Big Voice. I'm not saying that it will be easy. Time and again you've heard me say just how committed you must be to stay in your Big Voice. Practice your values and goals, and make a daily plan. Steer clear of those who will pull you away.

Growing yourself and your awareness should be an obsession. It brings so much joy and intention in your life that you may have lacked before. The opportunity to connect with like-minded people might seem daunting, but again you must be intentional about it. Your Little Voice will do its best to make you think it is too hard. The book stores and internet are chock-full of information. I wouldn't be who I am today without Oprah, Brené Brown, Marianne Williamson, Tony Robbins, Wayne Dyer, Jim Rohn, the Dali Lama, and many other thought leaders. I still believe it is a miracle that such a self-absorbed, small-town girl would have a calling to change the way women think and act. My purpose unfolded the way God intended it to.

When we find our Big Voice and authentic self, will we finally be free from suffering? It sounds amazing, but it is virtually impossible. You can minimize self-suffering but never eliminate problems or bad things from happening. After fifteen years of working on myself, I still have areas I want to get better at. If we can stay 100 percent in our Big Voice, it will not allow us to create our own suffering. If pain or sadness occurs, it will continue to fill us with joy. It is detached and knows we cannot avoid pain or loss in this world. It accepts the brokenness of this world and has the keen ability to always remain trusting of God.

I experienced this place of "nirvana" when my mom died. I had thirteen years to prepare myself for her death and because of that was able to find gratitude when it happened. I experienced incredible joy through her last years because I accepted her journey completely. My dad wanted to focus on all the negative changes she was going through while I viewed them differently. Accepting that our body ages and death is inevitable will release us from so much suffering. If you can believe your loved ones are going to heaven and you will meet again, your time without them on earth will fly by.

The shift in mindset that we need that knows we can get through suffering on earth by trusting

God will come from our Big Voice or authentic self. Our Little Voice wants to keep us paralyzed with blame, doubt, anger, and a lack of understanding. Our Big Voice knows we may never understand suffering but we can stay loving and joyful in spite of it.

As you realize that your Big Voice would never choose self-suffering, you can start seeing things more clearly. When you are discontent you can start recognizing you might not be in the right state. Overthinking or anxiety is caused by your Little Voice. This awareness allows you to make a shift and identify what you need to let go. Usually, you have some deep preference that is not lining up with reality. You will notice this is more likely to happen when you have too much on your plate or a lot of external problems that are weighing you down.

When you make a decision to believe that your true authentic self or Big Voice would never create suffering, you can detach from these thoughts and let them pass you by. It will change your life in the sense that patterns you have had forever will be broken. You will no longer hold onto thoughts or emotions that bring you down.

Since your Little Voice wants you to suffer, you will never be free until you learn how to recognize it and see what it's doing to you. I love Guy

Finley's analogy in *The Secret of Letting Go* where he describes your Little Voice as a psychic echo that keeps you discontent. Any painful event or trace of unhappiness produces an inner echo that is really just a phantom noise. He uses a story of a man lost in a cave that calls, "Hello" to himself and then goes deeper and farther from help because he follows his own echo. We can often get caught up chasing our Little Voice or ego without even realizing it.

It is possible to come to a point where you don't follow the echo. You have awareness to see it for what it is and find humor in it. Your Big Voice is always there if you stay present. I have found that sometimes I create my own suffering because I can't tell the difference between the Big and Little Voices and am struggling with a decision or situation. I get caught up trying to figure out what I should do. When I get curious about this I have found that if there is a possibility of hurting or disappointing someone, then my lower self or Little Voice focuses on my perfectionism instead of what is best.

I honestly have never met a human being that doesn't battle their highest and lowest self. Even the masters themselves will tell you that it can show up. It will keep us humble and ensure we constantly turn to God rather than believe we are perfect.

A Big Voice World

What would the world be like if you were a more powerful and balanced woman; if you embraced your Big Voice? I can imagine a place where all women are connected on a deeper level, are not suffering as much, and are being of service.

You would look and feel better as stress would diminish. You would be more rested and have more energy. Your relationships with your family would improve. You would pour your love and support into them unconditionally and without judgment or expectation.

You would not go through your days being critical of yourself. No more internal battle between your Little Voice and Big Voice. Your highest power would lead your life. You would have a deeper relationship with your Creator and would trust Him completely to guide you. You would let go of trying to control everything and everyone. You would surrender to the infinite possibilities of God's plan. You would begin to see your life as a masterpiece and yourself as beautiful and amazing. You would begin to honor your own spiritual health as being as important breathing. You would spend time caring for your spirituality and loving yourself.

With your newfound energy you will find God's purpose for your life and contribute to the world. You will laugh more and find the beauty all around you. Some of you may be founders of large corporations and others serving in a soup kitchen. You will all respect one another no matter what you are driven to do. You will invest your time and energy to help women and children that are suffering. You won't feed more suffering by self-loathing or giving other women permission to gossip and complain.

As you face life's unavoidable problems you will remain joyful through your suffering. You will not turn to distractions to avoid your pain or grief. You will accept thoughts and emotions cannot be controlled, but you will no longer allow your Little Voice to affect your feelings or actions. You will be more committed to your mindset and anything not in alignment with it will not have power in your life.

Being fully authentic and fearless, you will accomplish whatever you set your mind to. You will start spending more time on your highest priorities. You will create your vision and goals and no longer procrastinate or beat yourself up. If you can't prioritize something you will just move it farther out in your life, recognizing you have a delicate balance of things at which you can be good.

You will help the men in your life become more awake as well. You can teach them what you need and give them an opportunity to become the men God intended them to be. You will no longer steal their joy by your controlling ways or jealousy. You will not emasculate them or make them feel like they can never be enough for you. You will be grateful for their strengths and accept their weaknesses. You will help them become healthier and less distracted because your joy and energy will be contagious.

Your children will know the values and wisdom you want to teach them. You will show up present and intentional. You will not allow your biases to direct or guide their choices. You will see they need deadlines, standards, and boundaries and there will be seasons when they aren't appreciative.

You will demand higher standards in the food and drug industry. You will be more intentional about how you treat your body and fill it with healthier options. You will peel back the veil of convenience and distraction and realize your physical body must be put first. Your children will benefit by not consuming processed foods or an insane quantity of sugar. You won't give in to what they want because you will know the deceit that exists out there. You will lessen your schedule knowing it will keep you from burning out. You recognize that much of what others think important to do is meaningless.

You will know you need maximum energy to remain in your Big Voice. You won't take on too much and leave yourself depleted. You will prioritize your physical and emotional health over all else so you are vibrant and ready to take on whatever life hands you. You will celebrate any growth and success you have rather than focusing on wanting more.

You will be ready to help others in need all over the world. Although you each of you will serve different needs, you will no longer sit back and accept that evil just exists. You will stand up and fight for rights that every human deserves.

You will support women everywhere with love and acceptance and join your Big Voice with theirs. You will smile more and take more time to connect. You will live the amazing life you were born to live.

It is time, yours and mine and all of ours, to not only shatter the glass ceiling once and for all, but to take charge of our lives and leave our mark on a world that so desperately needs us.

"Never doubt that a small group of thoughtful, committed citizens can change the world. Indeed, it is the only thing that ever has." Margaret Mead

For help in writing a new story and learning to listen to your Big Voice, download the Big Voices Essential Tool Kit for free at: www.bigvoicesrise.com

ABOUT THE AUTHOR

Kelly Resendez wasn't always a success; at least not in her own mind. While others saw a woman who could do it all – a top producer, high-powered executive, tireless volunteer, a single mom raising strong, independent kids – Kelly was plagued by a feeling there was a larger purpose for her life. Naturally curious, she dedicated fifteen years to personal growth and development, studying under some of the masters of our day. When she finally surrendered to a higher power and found faith her purpose was revealed – to empower other women to embrace who they are, discover the joy that is theirs for the taking, and make the world a better place.

Kelly founded Big Voices Rise in 2017 with this purpose in mind. It is a standing invitation to women to join an empowered network whose mission is to positively impact lives by providing the tools and knowledge to think and respond differently, reduce suffering and increase joy, and become their true authentic self. Kelly has taken the best of what she has learned, those things that she herself applies every day to maintain joy, and shared it with others. She has coached and mentored hundreds of leaders and women in her career. Kelly is dedicated to helping women play a bigger game, have a bigger impact, and enjoy greater freedom, joy, and love.

Kelly holds the title of Executive Vice President for Paramount Partners Group, where she heads the retail mortgage division for Loan Pal. She uses the same concepts of mindfulness, self-discovery, and goal setting to help those in the mortgage and real estate industries create a successful business. She is the author of *Foundation to Sustainable Success: A Conscious Guide to Mastering the Mortgage Industry*. A frequent speaker who loves sharing wisdom with others, Kelly lives in California with her two teenaged children. She is an avid reader, life-long learner, and true believer in being good to your body so it will be good to you.

ACKNOWLEDGMENTS

To Paige and Cole: My precious children who helped me get this to the finish line. Your love and feedback are priceless and have helped me grow as a person and a mom every day.

To my mom and grandma in heaven: I miss you every day but feel your strength and love pouring into me. I learned so much from you both.

To my dad: You have been a wonderful dad and I am grateful for how close we are and the lessons I learned from you.

To my sister: I love you unconditionally and will never stop praying for your physical and emotional well-being. I am grateful for the support and love you have given me over the years.

To my nieces: You have shown me strength and courage through the most incredible experience ever. I am so proud of you and will always be here for you.

To Jay: I am forever grateful for you and your ability to co-parent our children in the most loving and supportive way. You are an amazing man and dad.

To Kirsten, Rebecca, Nicole, Angela, Andrea, Victoria, Traci, Katy, Amy, Cheryl, Cady and Rhonda: Your friendship has been invaluable to me. I love you all. Thank you for putting up with me while I was on this journey.

To Gloria, Jackie, and Bev: You have all stepped in and loved me like your own daughter at times. I smile every time I think of you.

To Theresa and Kathi: With your guidance, I continuously have grown through some of the hardest seasons of my life. Thank you for your wisdom, love, and nuggets that have been shared in this book.

To Caren: You have stood by me and guided me through this process. I could not have done it without you.

To the Team at PPG and Loan Pal: I can't begin to name you all but trust you know who you are. Thank you for loving me and supporting me.

To my Teachers: There are countless Pastors, authors, and speakers I could acknowledge. Many of you are quoted or referenced in these pages, but you were all there for me when I committed to writing a new story. Although I don't know all of you personally, you have shaped my ability to live an extraordinary life.

Made in United States
North Haven, CT
21 February 2024

49000519R00186